Ragged Road

Theresa Konwinski

ISBN: 0692842896
ISBN-13: 978-0692842898
LCCN: 2017902514

DEDICATION

Before the 1970s, many young, unwed, pregnant women were whisked away to remote locations, waiting out their pregnancy under the scrutiny of distant family or frequently, alone in a "maternity home." Sometimes the fathers of these babies were glad for the chance to be divested of responsibility. However, there was also a population of fathers who were never given an opportunity to know the child they had helped produce, and in terms of the law, there was little that could be done about it. Finding your child in those days was no easy task, desperate and frantic as some were to find their offspring. There was no DNA testing as we know it now. There were no computer records.

This book is dedicated to all the young mothers who gave up their children and the fathers who were not given a chance to know them.

This story offers no political commentary or answer. It's just a story.

THERESA KONWINSKI

ACKNOWLEDGMENTS

I've been fortunate to work with many of the finest nurses I could have ever hoped to know, only two of whom are Angi (*without an 'e'*) Sweeney and Deb White. They are both intelligent, compassionate, and have great instincts and common sense. Because I wanted to pay tribute to them, they allowed me to use their names in telling this story.

One of our most celebrated authors, Stephen King, has recommended that every author have an 'ideal reader.' Susan Anderson continues to be one of mine, and I appreciate her incredible patience with my processes.

Finally, when I get a crazy idea in the middle of the night, my husband, Frank, is the one I wake up to talk about it with, and what's more, he doesn't even mind. That's a best friend for you.

1

The River of Peace, as the Neuse River is known, harbors abundant life - catfish, shad, flounder, and delicacies like blue crab and oysters - a miracle, really, since a thick leafy canopy hides sections of the river from bright, clarifying shafts of light. Except for where the river runs through a narrow limestone gorge near Goldsboro, loose sandy banks outline the river from the place it is formed by the Flat and Eno rivers to where it reaches out for Pamlico Sound.

Old timers believe the dense green treetop crown holds in the river's secrets. From the displacement of the Neusiok Indians by white settlers and probably before, the river has heard the cries or laughter of young and old, swallowing confidences into the muddy bottom. Joys and heartaches of generations have washed into the water to be swept away or crashed on the rocks. The river leaves nothing behind.

Thinking about the river's two-million-year history and legends, Rafe Whitfield picked his way along the muddy banks looking for a good place to throw in his fishing line. Fishing was a way to draw inward for a while, to settle one's soul. Whether all that was known about the river was fact or fiction could be contemplated watching a bobber on top of the murky water.

Lanky and limber, he hopped over less desirable spots along the shore and selected a big flat rock. He sat down, putting his tackle box within easy reach. It was a lazy afternoon – no need to make work out of fishing. He loaded his hook and cast out into the middle of the river, which was flowing quickly today…it was hard to tell whether this would be a good or bad day for catching anything worth keeping. His red and white bobber performed a furious dance on the water; left, then right; up, then down. It was not easy to stay in control of the line in that kind of turbulence. The herky jerky of the bobber reminded him of the Lenoir County Winter Homecoming where he and Rose had danced a frenzy until damp with sweat. That dance had awakened feelings that led the young lovers to lose themselves in each other in the back of his Ford, a frenzied dance of another kind. He smiled at the memory. It hadn't been their first time, but nothing prior had surpassed that one night.

Could intensity of passion increase fertility? Rafe didn't know, but Rose had become pregnant. Although they were both seniors in the Class of '68, they were still not quite done with high school. Pregnancy was not the best news they could receive at this stage of life. It wasn't that Rafe didn't love Rose or want to marry her – they had talked about it several times - but neither of them had pictured it taking place this way. Rose had dreamed of a white gown and flowers and a reception in the grand old style of the Caswell family, maybe even under a big tent on the Caswell estate. Rafe had never been particularly interested in a lavish affair. As a middle-class boy, he had learned that keeping things low key was a better economic decision. Money was no object for the Caswells, but for the Whitfields it was a different story. Nevertheless, Rose…the queen of his heart…Rose fancied a grand event, equal to her family's name. Such an event would not be sensible or even possible now.

* * *

When Rose had originally told him she was pregnant, Rafe didn't know exactly what to think or how to feel. He was shocked, but shock soon gave way to a happy feeling that seemed odd given the circumstances. Today, he was making his case for marriage. They talked about it as they walked by the river later that afternoon.

"You know I love you. Let's get married right away," he said.

"I love you, too, but we've got to figure out how we're going to let our folks know about what's happened," she replied.

"Why? Let's just run off. We're of legal age to make the decision. I've got money saved up for college and we can get a license, get married, and start our life together."

Rose hesitated, deep in thought. "Rafe, you're a good man. But face it. Starting a marriage this way will not be easy. We love each other, but…" She left the comment hanging in the air and looked down at the ground.

"What is it? Out with it. We have to be honest with each other on this," Rafe encouraged.

"Daddy and Mother will have a fit if I just run off. They've been planning for me to go to State in the fall. This is going to be hard for them. You know my father. It's got to be his way, always. They will be mortified that their only daughter is pregnant out of wedlock. In their eyes, that's the worst possible sin. Girls who get pregnant out of wedlock are whores, sluts…I'll be an outcast in my family, my town."

"People are stupid and cruel. Forget them. Not your parents, of course, but the rest of them. Ok, Rose, I agree - we have to be honest with our parents. I know your dad has never been my biggest fan, but he'll get used to the idea once he sees that we really love each other and that we want to begin our life together. There's no reason you can't still go to State. Pregnant girls go to college. There's no stigma there. It happens all the time."

"You're naïve, Rafe. It *doesn't* happen all the time, especially to the Caswells. Family honor is at stake. I guarantee you – the discussion will be bloody. What about your folks? How are they going to take it?"

"I'm not sure. I imagine Mom will be hurt and Dad will just tell me I have to be a man and do the right thing, which is what I want to do anyway. But we don't have 'family honor' at stake. We're just poor white trash compared to your clan."

"Rafe, that's not fair and you know it. The Caswells have a responsibility to the community, have a reputation to maintain to help preserve Kinston's place in North Carolina's history. Why Daddy…."

Rafe interrupted, something he didn't usually do with Rose because he loved the sound of her voice and the rhythm of her words. "Rose, the Caswell name and the importance of Kinston to the state of North Carolina have long ago been diminished. You're talking about faded glory, girl. I'm not trying to be mean. I know your family feels the pressure of their heritage, and I don't fully understand it. But do you really think you are the first Caswell girl to get pregnant without a marriage license in place? *You're* the one whose naïve."

Rose was silent for a moment. She looked out over the brown and brackish river, then spoke so quietly Rafe could barely hear her over the rushing water.

"You may be right, but I know my father all too well. You have your eyes on the bright side. I have my eyes on the Caswell side, and that side is bright only so long as everything is perfect and in its place. We'll see, Rafe Whitfield. We'll see how things proceed from here."

He held her hand all the way back to the Ford, where he stopped long enough to hug her tight.

"You try not to worry so much, Rose. Worrying is not good for the baby. We're going to love this baby and raise it right here in Kinston. If anyone says anything cruel to our baby, they'll answer to me. If your parents don't understand, we'll show them by our actions. Love isn't something you put on a front about. Love isn't something for show. Love isn't about position and reputation. And we can't let any of that get into our minds. It won't be easy to break this news, but it has to be done. Let's tell my parents tonight and then talk to your parents on the weekend. What do you say?"

Rose looked him in the eye and answered, "You're brave. You're going to have to hold my hand the whole time or I'll just plain fall out, I know it. You've never seen Daddy when he's good and mad. I can't help it Rafe. For all your bravery, I'm scared to death. I don't know if I can get through it."

"We still have the option of eloping and just saying we had a 'honeymoon baby.' I'll leave with you tonight if you say the word," Rafe countered.

"No," she responded, suddenly firm. "No. That's cowardly, and I see that. We have to go forward on the truth." Her eyes were steely and determined.

"I'll pick you up at 7 o'clock. Wear your prettiest dress." Rafe smiled and kissed her lightly on the lips. "Jump in. It's almost time for you to be home from school. No need to set off any inquiries right now."

They got into the car and sped off for Caswell Farms, the biggest cotton farm in Lenoir County. Rafe dropped Rose at the bottom of the high-columned front porch steps.

"Love you...see you later," she said as she turned and started up the steps to the porch. She turned back to Rafe, leaned against a column and gave a little wave. Rafe blew her a kiss, then started back down the drive.

Near the end of the long lane, Rafe saw a small commotion off to the right in his peripheral vision. He slowed down and looked more carefully. Stuart Jefferson Caswell, Rose's older brother, was openly berating one of the farm hands. Rafe could see that his face was red, eyes bulging, and though Rafe couldn't make out his words, his voice was loud and angry. Rafe was a little afraid that Stuart was going to hit the farm hand, but surely Stu would know better than to pull such a stunt.

As he continued driving home, Rafe realized how unsettled the Stuart situation had left him. Stu had looked like a man gone berserk. God only knew what the farm hand had done or *not* done to deserve such a tongue lashing, but just wait till he heard about Rose. If this was any indication, Stu might be harder to tell than Rose's parents.

His mother was in the kitchen getting supper together when he walked in the door. She was an excellent cook, and Rafe knew he would miss her fine meals when he and Rose had a home of their own. Rose was not adept in the kitchen. She had never *had* to do much cooking because the Caswells employed a cook.

"Mother is far too busy with community charity work to spend time in the kitchen," Rose once told him. "My cooking skills could use some improvement, too," she had said, blushing.

That had never bothered Rafe. He knew how to cook a little and had always figured his own mom could teach Rose to cook if Rose wanted to learn. He had decided a long time ago that Rose would have the freedom to choose for herself. She wanted to go to State so she could have a career – cooking might never be her forte, and that was fine. Times were changing for women.

"Hey Rafe," his mother called out as he walked into the kitchen. "Been out with Rose?"

His mother liked Rose a lot. The two of them would sit and talk while he and his dad watched baseball or football on TV, and it seemed like the ladies couldn't have cared less that the men were otherwise preoccupied. Rose and his mom were like two old friends, really, and it made him happy. They were *connected*.

"What's for dinner, Mom? I'm starved."

"Pot roast with carrots and potatoes. Apple pie for dessert."

"What's up after dinner?" he asked. "Do you guys have anything planned?"

"No. Why?" Mom questioned.

"I thought I'd bring Rose over for a while and we could all spend the evening together."

Rafe's mother eyed him suspiciously. At least that's how it seemed to him…almost as if she already knew something was amiss.

"Well, it's still a school night so obviously you two can't be here real late, but of course you can bring Rose over. She's always welcome here." His mom smiled in a way that put Rafe's fears to rest.

"Great. I'm going to put my junk upstairs and I'll be back down to help you get things around," Rafe said.

"Well my, my. That's the first time you've offered to help in the kitchen for a while. I'll take you up on it."

Rafe went to his room and crashed on the bed for a few minutes. He knew in his heart of hearts that his parents would be disappointed that his married life was starting after a baby was already on the way, but they would never do anything like throw him out on his ear or threaten to not help with college, or so many of the other things he had heard guys talk about. He had known more than one older guy who had gotten a girl pregnant, but most of them had gone off somewhere to get rid of the child. Some went to see backwoods doctors who knew how to do abortions, either with a potion or sometimes with instruments. Rafe had heard tales of girls who were so badly butchered up they could never have a baby in the future, even if they wanted one. Other girls put their babies up for adoption. Only a very few of the unwed couples he knew had gotten married, and most of them didn't have a union that lasted long.

"That can't happen to us," he said to the ceiling. "That *won't* happen to us."

He jumped up, energized with the mission of protecting Rose and their child. He joined his mother in the kitchen and began to set the table. He moved automatically, lost in his own thoughts about how to find the right words to share the news with his parents.

After dinner ended and the dishes were done, Rafe went to pick up Rose. She was waiting for him on the front steps of the Caswell home, looking beautiful in a yellow dress. She barely waited for him to stop before she had her hand on the door handle.

"Let's get out of here," she said.

Rafe stepped on the gas and when they got to the end of the long driveway, he asked, "What's the matter? Why are you in such a hurry to 'get out of here'?"

"It's so horrible. Stu got in a fight with one of the farm hands today. Wesley Ammons - Stu beat him bloody. Then he fired him. He accused Wesley of stealing, which Wes denied, and Stu went crazy. Daddy's about to have a stroke; he's afraid Stu will be arrested."

6

"Oh, man. I saw that happening today when I dropped you off from school. I could tell that Stu was upset, but I never thought it would come to blows. I kind of wish I'd gone over and broken it up," Rafe said quietly. "I never would have dreamed…."

"You don't know Stu that well. He's a hot head for sure. If you lived with him every day of your life, you'd know what I mean," Rose answered.

"That doesn't make it any easier to tell your family about the baby. We're going to have to have a plan, I think." Rafe became quiet and concentrated on the road.

Rose was quiet, too, then said, "Maybe you're right about running away."

"Well, we're telling my parents tonight – right now – so we have to make a decision pretty quickly," Rafe said. "You know I'll do whatever you think is best."

Rose seemed to shrink back in the seat of his car. "No, no…I keep trying to take the chicken's way out. We're going to be fine, but it's just not going to be easy."

"Ok. The decision is made…no going back." Rafe reached over for Rose's hand. It was ice cold.

"Don't be nervous. My mom and dad love you and will be happy you're going to be their daughter-in-law. It might not be happening the way they wanted it, but they'll be ok." Rafe sounded more confident than he felt right at that moment.

"I hope you're right," Rose answered as they pulled into the Whitfield's driveway and parked the car.

Rafe opened the passenger side door and helped Rose out of the car. He gave her a quick kiss and put something in her hand.

"For luck," he said.

Rose smiled. It was a lovely glass pendant, containing a four-leaf clover. "For luck," she agreed.

2

They entered the house and the foyer was dark. Rafe's parents were in the living room with the lights low, watching "Gomer Pyle." Glenn Whitfield had been a Marine and loved the show. Anne Whitfield tolerated it.

"Hi, Mom and Dad," Rafe called cheerfully. "Look who's here."

Anne immediately got up and came over to Rose. "Hello, darling girl. Good to see you. Would you like some tea or some Coke?"

"Maybe just a glass of water with some ice in it tonight," Rose answered, and Anne disappeared into the kitchen.

"Well, young lady, that is a very becoming dress you're wearing." Glenn said. "Is it a special occasion?"

Rose sat down and glanced at Rafe, her face flushed. "Oh, no, it's just a dress I got in Wilmington."

"You look very nice," Glenn turned back to the TV as Anne returned to the room with a tray of glasses. She handed one to Rose, and Rose took a long sip.

Rafe anxiously reached for a glass, too – he almost knocked over the other glasses.

"Good grief son, be careful!" Anne said. "You'll spill water all over Rose."

Rafe laughed a nervous laugh and cleared his throat. "Can we turn the TV off for a little bit?" he asked.

"Well sure, I guess so." Dad hated to miss his favorite comedy, but got up and walked over to the TV. When he had pushed the 'off' button, he turned and looked at Rafe and Rose. "I get the sense that we're about to have an important discussion."

Rafe's dad knew him well. They were a lot alike in many ways, and he always could draw a bead on Rafe's emotional state without too much trouble.

"Well, yes, Rose and I have some important news to tell you and we really appreciate not having the TV on while we all talk," Rafe answered.

"You two are getting married!" Anne's face lit up in a smile. "You're getting married and going to State together."

"Well, you're at least partly right, Mom," Rafe said. "We definitely want to get married. We want to go to State. But there's more."

Anne and Glenn looked at the young couple, intent and quiet.

"Rose is pregnant, Mom and Dad. We know this is not the best news for you to hear tonight, but we wanted to be open about it. We *do* love each other, and we *do* plan to get married, but our schedule has been pushed ahead a little because Rose is going to have a baby." Rafe stopped talking. There was little else to say.

Anne Whitfield looked down at her hands. Rafe thought he saw a tear run down her cheek. Glenn looked at Rafe, then at Rose, apparently in shock. He stood up and started pacing back and forth. The room felt suddenly stifling.

"Well, well. Quite a predicament you two have gotten yourselves into. I'm not sure I know what to say," Glenn finally spoke.

Anne looked up from her hands. "You two know better. You've not been raised this way. That said, I think you should get married. I know you love each other, but you're still teenagers and have a lot to learn about each other and about marriage. You've painted yourselves into a corner, though. You must get married."

Glenn looked at his wife. "What makes you feel so certain that marriage is the best thing for the kids at this point?"

Anne took a sip of her water. "Truthfully, I'm *not* certain, but I also don't feel like there's much choice. That's just the way these things go. Rose's reputation will be ruined otherwise." She looked at Rose, realizing she had probably just hurt the girl. "I don't mean to sound uncaring or crude or hateful, Rose. I just know how gossipy this town can be, and I know what kind of impact this will have on your family."

"Mrs. Whitfield, you have never been anything but kind to me. I take no offense," Rose answered. "I can't see any other way, either, really, and Rafe feels the same way. We love each other."

"We do love each other, Mom and Dad. We know it won't be easy, we know we're young, but we also know we can make it work. Do you trust me on this?" Rafe looked at his father. "If I can be half the husband and father you are, I think we'll be all right."

Glenn crossed the room and put a hand on Rafe's shoulder. "Son, I'm proud of you - Rose, you too – for being honest and having the courage to tell us about this. I know you well enough to know that you can do anything you put your mind to. I think what we have to do now is start thinking about the practical things that must be accomplished. You two will get married, but you have to finish high school, you'll probably have to find a job and get insurance. You'll have to have a place to live...."

"Well, they can just live here," Anne spoke up. They can sleep right in Rafe's room. It will be nice having another female in the house." She smiled and crossed over to Rose, taking both her hands. "Darling girl, we think the world of you. Do you know you're not the first girl to get pregnant without being married? It happens. Try not to worry. Have you been to see the doctor?"

"Yes. I had to hide it from Mother and Daddy, though," Rose answered.

"They don't know yet?" Anne asked.

"No...not yet...we're trying to figure out how to break it to them. Daddy is very conscious of our family's reputation. I think he's going to take it hard. I dread telling him." Rose stood and looked Anne in the eyes. "He's not an easy man."

"Would you like us to go with you?" Anne looked over at Glenn, who nodded agreement.

"I'd have to think about that. He might be mad at me, but he might be even *more* mad if he thinks he wasn't the first to find out. I would have to think it through," Rose said.

"Once you decide, you just let us know," Glenn offered. "We'll do anything we can to help you. You're family now."

"Thank you both for how you've taken this news," Rafe said. "It's not the kind of news we wanted to have to tell you, but it's the situation at hand. It's kind of scary. We need our parents more than ever so we can start moving forward in our life together."

"And so it shall be," Anne said. "It's getting a little late and you should probably get Rose back home now. Rose, try not to worry. These things often work themselves out in ways you would never expect."

"Thanks, Mrs. Whitfield," Rose started, but Anne interrupted.

"How about calling me Anne?" she asked.

Rose smiled for the first time that evening. "I'd like that. Thank you."

Rafe and Rose walked out the front screen door and down one step off the porch onto the sidewalk. They walked slowly and quietly to the car, hand in hand, contemplating what they had just accomplished and what they had yet to face.

3

"You know Ham Caswell as well as just about anyone in this town, Glenn. How do you think he's going to react to all this?" Anne and Glenn sat on the front porch after the kids left. A cool spring breeze blew like a whisper. It seemed natural to talk in hushed tones about what they had just learned.

"I can tell you unequivocally what will happen. He'll be mad as a hornet. He'll blow a gasket. He'll kick Rafe right out of the house. And then he'll beat Daisy because she didn't teach Rose right from wrong, even though she did, of course," Glenn answered.

"God in heaven. Do you really think he'll go that crazy? He loves Rose within an inch of his life. Everyone knows that. His kids are his crown," Anne said.

"Yes. But only after the Caswell heritage." Glenn closed his eyes for a minute. "I remember when we were all in high school...Ham Caswell – descendant of Richard Caswell, first governor of North Carolina...at least that's what he always told us. Whole family gobbled up into politics and most of it dirty. But Ham wasn't a terrible person...he just had a name and he tried to use it to his advantage. We got along all right. I did try to keep the peace with him, that's for sure. He was a killer on the football field. He used us as tackling dummies to take out his aggressions. It wasn't till later in life that he got so out-and-out mean. Everyone in town knows Daisy's his tackling dummy now, but I don't know that there's much anyone can do about it."

"Do you think he's an alcoholic? I've seen him put away a lot of liquor at public events," Anne said. "Maybe he beats Daisy after he's had too much to drink."

"I have a feeling alcohol has nothing to do with it, though it may loosen him up a bit. I think he's nasty whether he's drunk or sober. He's just crazy mean now."

"Well, we better warn Rafe about that. I don't know if he's ever seen Ham when he's really mad. As it is, I suspect he's just tolerated Rafe. Now he's going to have him for a son-in-law. "

"Annie, my dear, you're an optimist. I'm praying Ham will handle the news like a man, but I'm not holding my breath."

"Do you think we should go with them when they talk to Ham and Daisy? Maybe having other people there will help him stay in control."

Glenn leaned back and put his hands behind his head. "You heard Rose tonight. She's got to think on that one. I feel like we should follow her lead. If she says 'please come with us,' I'll be there. Otherwise, we need to stay out of the kids' way."

They pushed the swing back and forth a few times, considering the moon. It was just a crescent, a silver sliver in the sky. Clouds obscured its light at times, then moved silently away.

"Rain. We're supposed to get some rain," Glenn said.

They picked themselves up to head in for the night, taking one last glance up at the sky.

"Don't worry, mama," Glenn said. "It will all work out all right. This is not the first time kids have gotten themselves in trouble; it won't be the last. Rafe is a good boy and Rose is a good girl. I have every confidence in the two of them together."

"I hope you're right," Anne whispered, leaning into Glenn's arms. "I sure hope you're right."

4

Rose put on her yellow dress – the one Mr. Whitfield had said looked so nice on her. She wanted her own father to see her in that same light. The dress felt a little snug in the waist already. She really hadn't noticed till now that her belly was starting to push out.

"98, 99, 100." She finished brushing her long hair and put in the pearl earrings her father had given her for her 18th birthday, just a month before. Her hands shook slightly as she fastened the backs of the earrings. She looked at herself in the mirror and tried to calm herself by taking a deep breath and blowing it out slowly, then repeating the process several times. It didn't really seem to help.

"Dear God," she prayed quietly, "If you're listening to me this morning, please help me. I'm scared. I know I made a mistake, but please help my parents understand and forgive me. Help me and Rafe be strong and brave and be good parents to this little baby."

She looked back up into the mirror. She didn't see a strong, brave girl. She felt nauseous. She put on her four-leaf clover necklace. *For luck,* she thought.

She heard a car pull up and the motor shut off. That would be Rafe, arriving for brunch. Today they would tell her parents about the baby. She got up and headed down the stairs.

Miss Stella, the Caswell's maid, was escorting Rafe into the sitting room when Rose got to the bottom of the steps. Miss Stella liked Rafe and always seemed flirty with him, though she was at least thirty-five years his senior. Miss Stella had been born in the hills of West Virginia, had grown up poor, and regularly told Rose how proud she was to work "for a fine family like the Caswells." She had never been married, and her attempts at flirtation were amusing to Rose. The scene momentarily lifted her spirits.

As she walked into the sitting room, Rafe rose from his chair and walked over to hug her.

"You two make a beautiful couple," Miss Stella gushed. "One day I 'spect to hear that we're plannin' a weddin'."

Rose and Rafe both smiled, but said nothing.

"Uh-huh. Silence is stronger than words," Miss Stella said as she left the room.

"Darlin', are you ready for this?" Rafe asked. "I didn't sleep worth a darn last night."

"Me either, but I suppose I'm as ready as I'll ever be. This dress is getting a little tight, and that means it won't be long before I'm showing. We have to get this over with whether we're ready or not," Rose replied.

"Ok. So here we go, and God help us," Rafe chuckled. "Maybe the anticipation is the worst part."

"Maybe…" Rose trailed off.

They went into the dining room where the table was beautifully laid out as if a party were taking place. Hamilton John Caswell was already at the head of the table, drinking coffee and reading the morning paper. He barely glanced up, muttering, "Good morning."

"Good morning, Daddy," Rose walked over to hug him. "Is there any good news in that paper you're reading?"

"Not much to speak of. The Dow Jones is up a little at close of day yesterday. That's about it." Hamilton always paid close attention to money.

"Good morning, Mr. Caswell," Rafe now spoke up. "I'm glad to be invited to brunch."

Ham looked over the top of his paper briefly. "Yes, well have a seat. I'm sure the food will be out here before too long."

Before Rafe could sit, Daisy Caswell walked into the room and crossed over to hug her daughter.

"Hello, sweet child." Daisy smiled and gushed in sing-song, "Rose, the darling of my heart, if God is in Heaven we shall never part."

"Mother, I'll always be your child, but I'm kind of grown up for that little song now. I'm graduating in a couple of weeks," Rose lovingly chided her.

"I know, and in the fall, you'll be off to North Carolina State and we'll barely see you. Let me enjoy you while I still have you." Daisy sat next to Ham and poured a cup of coffee.

Rose and Rafe glanced at each other, then joined Daisy and Ham at the table.

"Would you care for some coffee?" Daisy offered to Rose, then to Rafe.

"No, Mom, I'm more in the mood for some milk this morning," Rose said.

"I'll gladly have some coffee," Rafe spoke up. "Strong and black, please."

"Well, I can't attest to the strength of the coffee yet, but I can withhold the cream," Daisy smiled. She had always been friendly to Rafe, even if she didn't believe he was the best match for Rose. She had always favored David Teachey, the son of their best friends. David seemed to offer a more promising future, being from a prominent and wealthy family. Rafe was a nice boy, but as a mother, she had to look out for her daughter's future.

Ham folded and put down his paper, just as Miss Stella brought in brunch on a wheeled cart. As she was placing the food on the table, Ham asked, "So, Rafe. Your whole future is ahead of you. Have you decided what you are going to do with it?"

Nothing like taking the direct route, Rafe thought to himself.

"Well, sir, you're right. My whole future is ahead of me. Just like Rose, I've been planning to go to State in the fall. I got my acceptance letter about a month ago. I'm not sure what studies I'll take up, but I'll just start with general stuff and figure it out from there."

"That doesn't sound like much of a plan," Ham bluntly stated. "I'd think by now you'd have developed an idea of what line of work you'd be interested in when you are done with college. Then you would be able to focus all your studies in that field."

"I wish I had your traits of decisiveness and certainty, sir. I've surely given it a lot of thought. I can tell you that I'm very interested in journalism, and I'm also very interested in history, but I haven't decided anything for sure yet." Rafe felt the heat of Hamilton's glare and took a sip out of his water glass before continuing. "Unfortunately, neither of these areas of study will lead to great wealth, but my father has always told me to choose to make a living at something you love, and it will never seem like work."

"Nothing wrong with work," Ham grunted.

"Oh, of course not. I didn't mean…." Rafe didn't know how to end his sentence without sounding like he was trying too hard. He shoved a fork full of scrambled eggs in his mouth. This was not going as well as he would have hoped.

"I love the written word, and Daddy, I know how proud you are of our history. Either one of these fields would be wonderful areas for Rafe to study," Rose defended.

Ham didn't say any more, but began eating his brunch. Daisy glanced nervously around the table and began twittering about some social event she had attended that week. Rose and Rafe ate little, mostly pushing food around on their plates.

When Ham had finished his food, he pushed his chair back and lit a cigar. "Nothing like a fine cigar to end a meal," he said. "Rafe, do you take a cigar?"

"No sir, I never could get the gist of smoking anything, but thank you anyway."

"I wasn't offering," Ham growled as he got up and walked over to a window to look out upon the grounds of his estate.

Rose was anxious to move the conversation along – she couldn't stand the sense of dread one more minute. "Mother and Daddy, Rafe and I have something to tell you."

Rafe looked at Rose, not expecting her to jump into it this quickly.

"Yes, and what would that be?" Ham turned back to face the trio still seated at the table.

"Rafe and I are getting married," Rose said weakly, withering somewhat under Ham's glare.

"What do you mean 'married'?" Ham boomed. Daisy was sitting very still with her mouth hanging open, eyes wide.

"Just what I said. We're getting married." Rose became braver the more she spoke, and the words came in a rush. "Rafe is already nineteen and I'm eighteen, we're both graduating from high school, and we're both going to State. We're getting married before we go."

"Like blazes you are!" Ham strode over to the table and towered over Rose and Rafe. "You are too young to get married. Young people who get married right out of high school never get college completed. Look at me and your mother. Why do you think I never finished college?" Ham was shouting, and Daisy looked crushed by his inferences.

"Daddy, please lower your voice, calm down, and try to understand. I love Rafe and he loves me. We want to be together all the time. We know what we have ahead of us and we want to get married and share our experiences together," Rose continued. "You can't stop us. We're of legal age."

Ham's voice took on a sinister tone. "You really don't know what I can or can't do."

Rose looked for a second like she had been slapped. She grabbed Rafe's hand under the table, took a deep breath and said, "You may want to reconsider your position on this. I'm pregnant."

The room was deadly silent. Rafe's eyes were glued to Hamilton. He could not move his gaze away from the red-faced man who would soon be his father-in-law. He didn't see Daisy get up from the table and start backing away. He felt Rose squeeze his hand until he thought she might break it. That pulled him out of his frozen fear.

"Sir, I know this is not what you would have liked to hear from us this morning, but it's true. I have loved Rose for more than a year now and have known for a while that she was the girl I wanted to marry. This just moves our plans ahead a little and..." Rafe suddenly stopped as Ham glowered at him and began to move closer. Rafe thought it might be wise to stand up, and when he did, Ham moved his own face in close to Rafe's.

"There will be no marriage. Our daughter has a future that will never include you. How dare you put your hands on her and then come into my house to tell me you've impregnated her? How dare you? You will never amount to anything, and my daughter will not be saddled to a man who doesn't even know what he wants to do in life. You will leave this house now and I never expect to see you here again. Do you understand me? Don't ever even think about coming on this property or...."

"Daddy! Stop it right now! Rafe has done nothing that I wasn't a willing participant in. Stop it or you'll never see me again, either," Rose screamed.

With one hard blow, Hamilton John Caswell knocked his own daughter to the floor. Rose began to cry and Daisy whimpered in a corner of the room.

"Get out!" Ham bellowed at Rafe. "Get out before I kill you!"

Rafe walked over to Rose to help her up.

"Don't you touch her! Get out!" Ham was almost on top of him now.

"Rafe, please go...get out before he does something crazy," Rose cried.

Rafe straightened his shoulders, unafraid now of anything Ham could do to him. "This isn't your decision, Mr. Caswell, and if you hit Rose again, I'll have you arrested. I *should* have you arrested right now. Rose, I'll see you at school Monday morning. We'll talk then."

"We'll see about that," Ham said, putting himself between Rafe and Rose.

Rafe went out the way he had come in, bustling past Miss Stella, who had been standing outside the dining room. She looked like a scared rabbit.

"Mr. Rafe, are you all right? You better git on out of here right quick," she said.

"Good-bye Miss Stella. Thank you for breakfast," Rafe said as he opened the door and walked out into the sunshine. The warmth helped loosen up his muscles, which he now realized had been taut throughout the whole conversation with Ham and Daisy.

Before Rafe could get down the steps, Stuart Caswell pulled up to a lurching, screeching stop in front of the house. It was almost noon, yet he tumbled out of his car, disheveled and uncoordinated, his eyes bloodshot. Probably out drinking all night, Rafe thought. Like father, like son.

"Hey Rafe, come on in and have a beer with me," Stuart mumbled.

"Not a good idea, Stu," Rafe said, forcing a sickly smile. "I'll see you later." He got away from Stu as fast as he could, jumped in his car and headed for home. He didn't want to think about what was going on in the Caswell house by this time. Poor Daisy. Poor Rose. He glanced up in his rear-view mirror and saw Stuart still trying to open the front door.

5

Stuart Caswell had picked a bad morning to come home half drunk. He bumbled his way past Stella, who was still outside the dining room door. She looked like a whipped dog. Stuart could hear loud voices – mostly his father – coming from the dining room. He opened the door and stepped just inside.

Ham was helping Rose up off the floor and screaming at Daisy, who was whimpering in the corner. His mother had no spine at all. He shook his head in disgust at her inability to handle any stress, especially when it came to his father.

"Well, well, well. What's up with y'all?" Stuart asked mockingly. "Y'all havin' a party without me? Rose, why you on the floor? One too many?"

Rose pulled away from Ham as fast as she could and headed for the door where Stuart was standing. "Stu, you better watch your step today. He's in his usual foul humor and he's not happy with me right now…" she turned to face Ham "…because I'm pregnant as the day is long and I'm going to get married."

"What? Little Rose is going to have a baby rosebud? Well, isn't that something! My little sister going to have a baby," Stu slurred. "Guess you didn't see that one coming, Daddy."

"Keep your mouth shut, you drunk. What kind of family did I raise?" Ham turned to Daisy and began his tirade all over again. "If you were any kind of mother, she would have known to keep her legs together, but I guess the sins of the mother come home to roost in the daughter. The least you could have done is teach her how to prevent getting pregnant!" Ham was on a roll. Daisy cowered in her corner.

"I have tried to be a good mother," Daisy half whispered. "I have tried to teach her right. You can't control children. They have minds of their own."

"I'm surprised you have the nerve to even answer me right now," Ham said menacingly. "You and I will be discussing this later, out of the presence of the children." He turned back to Rose and Stuart. "Rose, go to your room. I have to think about what we're going to do about all this."

"I'll tell you what we're going to do, Daddy. Rafe and I are going to get married. You can't stop us. We are in love. Otherwise, this wouldn't have happened. You can't blame Mother, either." For all her earlier anxiety, Rose had found her voice and was not about to back down.

"It's time for you to close your smart mouth, young lady. I'll call you down from your room when I'm ready to talk to you anymore about this." Ham had taken a quieter tone, but was no less threatening. He had already moved on to calculation and scheming in his own mind.

Rose turned and left the room. As she walked up the staircase to the second floor, she suddenly became weak in the knees. Her father was a powerful man. She loved her father, but she was also scared of what he could do when he had a notion. He had always favored her, so she understood why he was hurt. Maybe they could talk to each other more when he wasn't so emotional. She said a silent prayer for her mother, knowing what Ham was capable of. Her mother had shown up to church or lunch with her lady friends with bruises and scrapes more than once. Rose was sure the other women knew what her mom endured, but no one, including Rose or Stu, knew how to help her.

She walked into her room, stretched out on the bed and looked up at the ceiling. Her ceiling fan still had the guardian angel pull chain from her childhood.

"I need you now, Guardian Angel. I need you to help me through all this." She closed her eyes and remembered the look on Rafe's face after her father had knocked her down. He looked scared, but she knew somehow that Rafe would always find a way to protect her. It was a comforting thought.

Downstairs, Stuart had settled down to a cup of coffee. His stomach wouldn't allow more than that right now unless he wanted to bring it all back up later.

Daisy had slithered out of the room and his father was standing in front of the French doors that led out to the stone patio. They had put that patio in with their bare hands, using field stones they had found on their property. It was the site of many family get-togethers and political fundraisers.

"Beautiful morning, eh, Daddy?" Stu looked for a way to engage his father in something other than a yelling match.

"It *was*," Ham growled. "It was before your sister made a mockery of her upbringing."

"Daddy, you have got to get over that. Rose is a young woman with a mind of her own. She's not your possession, you know." Stu was the only person who could get away with such talk. "You can own a lot of land and I know you own a lot of people, but you can't own Rose. She's always been a unique individual, I guess you could say."

"Mind of her own or otherwise, she has no business bringing that no-account son of a garage mechanic into my home and telling me he's the father of her illegitimate baby."

"Now Daddy, why would you even say something like that? You went to high school with Glenn Whitfield, didn't you? You've always been friendly with him." Stu was trying in his own way to find neutral ground, bring about peace for that Saturday morning.

"Yes, I'm friendly with him. He keeps the cars running for a good price. Being friendly is how you work with people. It's how you achieve certain ends. If you had any interest in our family's political history, you'd know this by now." Ham could never understand why his only son didn't show more interest in his heritage.

"Daddy, I've never had a notion to get involved in that world, so don't start on me about it now. The subject is Rose and how you're going to help her."

"She wouldn't have needed my help if she had behaved as a lady. I know someone who'll be able to help…I just have to make some calls. I've already got a plan brewing…and son, speaking of brewing, try not to make every Friday night a date with Jim Beam. If you'll excuse me…." Ham strode from the room, headed for the library, which also served as his home office.

Stu laughed and hiccupped, leaned back in his chair, picked up a piece of bacon from the table and started to put it to his lips. The very smell nauseated him and he put it back down on the serving plate and half-smiled. Ham and bacon definitely would not make for a good combination this morning.

6

Hamilton Caswell leaned back in his desk chair and surveyed his notes. The office was quiet except for the ticking of the grandfather clock he had inherited from his mother and father. He had insisted that it always be located in his office, though Daisy had a hissy fit that it wasn't placed in the formal living room. He felt an odd sense of fulfillment, and he didn't know if it was because he had won the battle of the grandfather clock or maybe because of what he had just accomplished on the phone.

He thought about what his own father would say about Rose. In his younger years, Ham had not been brave enough to tell his old man that Daisy was pregnant. Instead, he and Daisy had eloped. His father had been shocked, but if he guessed the reason for the sudden marriage, he had never confronted Ham about it. Ham still felt some sense of surprise about this…his father had been a cruel man, subject to fits of rage and hard punishments. Ham knew he could have been disinherited.

He pulled himself back to the present, put the notes he had taken in a manila folder and placed the folder in his top desk drawer. He locked it, pocketed the key, got up and walked over to the window. Wincing, he thought about how Rose would be viewed by his friends. His precious baby girl…she had always been the apple of his eye, the light of his life, and now this….

"She's no longer a girl," he said to no one, "but she'll not be a mother."

* * *

In another room of the mansion, Daisy Caswell cried for her daughter. After all the years of staying married to a harsh, controlling, abusive man, she had held on to dreams of a better life for Rose, who had grown up smart, kind, and beautiful, despite what she saw in her parents.

Daisy had endured a lot for the sake of her children. Now Stuart was a barely-functional drunk, trying and failing to live up to the expectations his father had for him. Rose was probably doomed to a life of spare means; a life of children and housework when she had hoped for a career and a life separate from the burdens of the Caswell name, a life away from Kinston. At least Rafe was a nice boy. His life just didn't hold the promise Daisy had hoped for her beloved daughter. Coming from a desperately poor background herself, she knew what it meant to scrape for every dime; to not be sure where the next meal was coming from; to have one thin coat, no matter the weather. Her own dear mother had dreamed big dreams for Daisy, and those were the things Daisy had imagined for Rose. Rafe would make something of himself – Daisy knew this – but like Stuart, he would also have a hard time living up to Caswell expectations.

She opened her Bible and read a few passages. She prayed for her children. She prayed for herself…she knew before long, she would be the one bearing the evidence of Ham's rage.

* * *

Stuart Caswell retired to his room to get some sleep. The night before had been long and rowdy. Stuart had always had a lot of friends as long as he was buying, and Friday had been payday; his so-called friends were quick to be at his side while the whiskey was flowing and they weren't paying for it.

He lay on his bed, but his thoughts wouldn't allow him to sleep. His sister had forever been the lamb of the family, especially to him. All throughout their childhood, he had tried to protect her from what he had so frequently been witness to – the beating of their mother by their own father. Stuart shook his head, remembering some of the thrashings his mother had withstood, his father in a blind rage about something of little consequence to anyone but him. Stuart never understood it – why his father would behave in such a way; why his mother would put up with it. His parents had a complicated relationship, and for as long as he could remember, he had tried to protect his baby sister from that truth. Oddly, Miss Stella seemed to be the only one who could mend the rift between his folks after such

24

an event. How did she hold his parents together? He couldn't understand it. Miss Stella was a meek little thing, but she always got Daisy back on her feet and Ham back in control.

And now Rose was pregnant. Rafe was clearly upset when Stu encountered him on the steps. He surely had seen Rose get knocked right down to the floor by their own father, something even Stu had never seen in all his life. Daisy, as usual, had cowered in the corner, no help to anyone. Stu wondered about how Rose and Rafe would ever get past Ham's indignation and put together a decent life. He had given up on such a life for himself, but he had never given up on Rose, and he fell asleep thinking about how he never would.

7

On Sunday morning, Rose was awakened by her father. "Get up and get dressed. You're going for a ride," he commanded. Half asleep, she glanced at the clock – 4 a.m. – then blindly followed his direction, brushing her teeth, washing her face, throwing on some old jeans and a blouse. She found him waiting at the bottom of the stairs, impatiently pacing back and forth in front of a suitcase, which brought her fully-awake. She felt some concern at the sight of that suitcase and walked down the steps slowly, wondering if the fate that awaited her was the same as that she had heard of before…girls getting sent off to "spend the summer with an aunt." That's what everybody always said.

"Get on down here. It's time to go," Ham said. He was stern, steely-eyed, and emotionless. He picked up the valise and opened the front door. "You're going to your Aunt Marnie's."

Mr. Jensen, the family driver, was waiting beside the Cadillac, which was parked with the motor running. Shocked beyond words, she followed her father out to the car, afraid to do anything else, her mind racing with how to get out of this. Mr. Jensen put her suitcase in the trunk and opened the automobile's back door for her.

"Daddy," she started to say, but her father had already turned to head back up the steps to the house. He spun around to interrupt her.

"You have made this mess, but I am fixing it. I'll provide for your needs and send you money when you run out. Otherwise, we will not be seeing you until this episode is over." With that, her father continued into the house and she watched in stunned, sleepy silence as the door closed behind him.

Mr. Jensen gave the smallest bow, an indication that she should get in the car, and she did. Mr. Jensen got behind the wheel and started down their long driveway. Rose turned to look out the back window, her home still dark and lifeless at this time of the morning. Her eyes began to fill with tears.

"How could he? How could he?" she muttered.

"Did you say something, Miss Rose?" Mr. Jensen asked, looking up at her in his rearview mirror.

"No, nothing, Mr. Jensen," she answered. She lay down across the back seat and cried quietly, trying very hard to muffle any sound.

Going to Aunt Marnie's wasn't the end of the world. Aunt Marnie was completely different from her father; kind, down-to-earth, not one to put on airs about the family name. Rose knew she would still be able to contact Rafe, let him know where she was. Maybe he could come to see her...perhaps they could marry in Chicago.

Eventually, she fell asleep. Riding in cars had done that to her since she was little, and it was a reprieve from the pain and - truth be told - the guilt she felt about this whole situation. Sleep was a blessing.

When she awoke again and sat up to look out the window, she was in no part of the country she had ever seen before.

"Mr. Jensen, where are we? I thought we were going to Chicago to my Aunt Marnie's," Rose queried.

"Miss Rose, my orders do not include Chicago."

Now a fear gripped her that she had never felt before, like a cold hand squeezing her heart. She had difficulty pulling in a breath.

"What exactly do your orders include, then?" she sputtered.

"Miss, I'm not to say until we arrive. Mr. Ham would kill me if I disobey his orders." Mr. Jensen seemed almost apologetic.

"Mr. Jensen, if you don't stop this car, I'll open the door and jump out!" Rose cried.

"Miss Rose, you don't want to do that. Just let me take you where you're supposed to go. People there will help you figure out the best thing to do from then on. Please, please don't do anything rash. You must not hurt yourself, *please*."

Rose sat back against the seat, her mind going a hundred miles an hour. What had her father cooked up this time? She couldn't begin to imagine, and in the absence of information, her fears got the best of her. She began to heave. There was nothing in her stomach but bile, which she vomited up, choking on the bitterness. She tried to vomit into her hands, but her blouse was stained with the green she had spewed up.

"Miss Rose, are you all right? There are tissues back there if you need to clean up," Mr. Jensen said to her without ever slowing down the car. They were sailing along at the speed limit. It was clear that nothing would stop him from delivering her wherever he was supposed to take her.

Rose looked at her stained blouse and began to cry - at first, a whimper; then, her body racked with great, heaving sobs. She felt helpless, hopeless, imprisoned. She cried for herself, she cried for her baby, and she cried for Rafe. The fact that her own father had done this to her was more than she could bear....

She found the tissues and dried her eyes, then tried to clean up her face and blouse as best she could. Mr. Jensen looked at her in the rearview mirror again and asked, "Are you feeling better, Miss?"

She didn't even feel like answering, but muttered, "I guess so." She scooted to the other side of the back seat so that Mr. Jensen couldn't see her so easily and tried to think.

I can't keep crying and being a baby, Rose thought to herself. *I'm a smart woman. I will figure out what to do. If only I knew where we were going, I could plan better. Never mind that. I'll figure it out when I get there. I'll figure it out, find Rafe, and then I'll never set foot in my father's house again. He can keep his money – give it to Stu, I don't care. All I want is Rafe and my baby. We'll have a better life on our own.*

At that very moment, Rose saw a sign. WELCOME TO WINCHESTER. Winchester! She didn't know a soul in Winchester, and to her knowledge, neither did her father. She had heard of it, of course, and knew its reputation as a lovely little town in the Shenandoah Valley, but what in God's name would she be doing here?

She started seeing street signs and tried to read them, just to hear the names. Martinsburg Pike. Cork Street. Jubal Early Drive. Mr. Jensen had slowed down and was looking at street signs, too, trying to find his next turn. Finally, they pulled onto a street called Fremont. Mr. Jensen drove even slower now, looking. It gave Rose a chance to get a sense of this town and to try to figure out what she was in for. The town was beautiful, really. There were huge maple trees lining Fremont Street, and everything was clean, neat, and orderly.

The car stopped in front of an older brick home. It was three stories, as best Rose could tell. Tall white columns reminded her of her own home, and she felt a twinge...her mother would be up and thinking about her pregnant daughter by this time. They had been driving almost six hours…it was nearly 10 a.m.

Mr. Jensen opened the door for her and offered his hand to help her out. Rose accepted because her legs felt wobbly and she was still nauseated. It was only then that she noticed a sign off to the right, almost hidden in some shrubs: CORDELIA WEINGARTEN HOME. Rose knew where she was. She began to shake.

"Come on, now, Miss Rose. Everything is going to be fine. These people will be able to take good care of you," Mr. Jensen encouraged.

"You can't be leaving me here, Mr. Jensen. Please, take me somewhere else. I won't tell Daddy. Please, you can't leave me here." Nearly begging, Rose tried pulling away from Mr. Jensen's firm grip. He put his arm around her waist and began walking towards the home, bringing her along. She felt too weak in the knees to resist in any real sense of the word and stumbled along with him.

"Miss Rose, you know I can't do that, and anyway, where would you go? These people deal with young pregnant ladies all the time and know what is best for you. Your father is trying to protect you. You have to accept this – it's his gift to you." Mr. Jensen kept moving forward, pulling her along.

"Oh, no, no…this is not a gift…." Rose trailed off.

"You'll soon come to see that it's for the best," Mr. Jensen said as they arrived at the front door. He pushed the door open and they stepped inside into a cavernous foyer. The floor was black and white marble, like a checkerboard. Off to the right, a swooping spiral staircase hinted at the grandeur the home once enjoyed. Rose could picture young debutantes coming down the staircase in their hooped ballgowns with a dozen Rhett Butlers waiting at the bottom. Everything was clean and bright – sunlight, filtered by the maple trees, poured in through large windows. There was a sitting room to the left in what appeared to have once been a sun porch. Just interior to the sitting room was an office door with a name plate: MRS. KELLOGG. They approached the door and Mr. Jensen knocked. Rose had an impulse to run away as fast as she could, but she knew Mr. Jensen was right. Where would she go? She was caught like a little rabbit.

The door opened, and a small, somber-looking woman said, "How may I help you?"

Mr. Jensen answered. "This is Miss Rose Caswell. I believe you all are expecting her."

"Yes, indeed. Come right in Miss Caswell. I am Mrs. Kellogg." The woman never smiled or extended her hand except to indicate a chair for Rose to sit in.

"I'll go retrieve your luggage, Miss Rose," Mr. Jensen said, turning to go to the car.

Rose followed Mrs. Kellogg across the room, observing the furnishings, the Persian rug, the expensive vases. The air carried a faint smell of cleaning substances. On one wall were black and white photographs of babies; the entire wall was nearly covered. Babies with little balled-up fists, babies with their eyes closed, some with their eyes open. There were pictures of babies of every different ethnic background you could name. Rose wondered where all those babies and their parents might be.

She sat down in an overstuffed chair and faced Mrs. Kellogg's desk. Mrs. Kellogg sat opposite Rose and pulled a file from a desk drawer. She opened it and looked at some papers for a minute before speaking again.

"Miss Caswell, I understand that you are now about four months pregnant. That means you are in your second trimester. Typically, the second trimester is one of good energy for pregnant young women. They are having less nausea and vomiting, resting better at night and so forth. This is the period when you will feel the baby starting to move." Mrs. Kellogg looked very intensely at her. "You will become less emotionally labile." She paused for a moment, then continued. "Your father, through the many important contacts he has, found our home and sent you here for the duration of your pregnancy. As a resident of the Weingarten home, you will have the best medical care available and you will be able to make friends with other young women in your situation. There are expectations you will be required to comply with."

"And what exactly would those 'expectations' be?" Rose asked, suddenly annoyed with Mrs. Kellogg's imperious manner.

Nonplussed, Mrs. Kellogg answered, "I'll provide you with a list once we have you settled in your room. I imagine your chauffeur has returned with your baggage by now." She got up and went to the office door. Rose followed. Her luggage had been placed on the floor right outside the office door, and Mr. Jensen was gone. Any opportunity to escape was gone with him.

"Pick up your suitcase and I'll show you to your room." Rose did as she was instructed, not wanting to come across as a troublemaker to this severe woman. She was starting to get a feel for what the next five months might be like.

They walked up the staircase, and on the second floor, Rose saw a few girls going in and out of what she assumed to be their own rooms. They were at various stages of pregnancy, some appearing to be nearly full-term. Mrs. Kellogg marched down the hall, nodding her head at the girls, but never speaking to any of them. Rose could see that it was all business with her.

She finally arrived at the very last door on the left side of the hall. Mrs. Kellogg unlocked the door and opened it. Rose was relieved to find a room of adequate space, with two large windows, a twin bed, two nice sitting chairs and a desk. She could see two closets and two chests – one on either side of the room. The room was clean and appeared to be comfortable. *A comfortable prison*, Rose thought to herself.

"Your father has made very gracious accommodations for you, Miss Caswell," Mrs. Kellogg said. "He wants only the best for you, and to the extent we are able to offer it, the best is what you shall have. You are the only girl here who has a private room, so you should be grateful to your father for that. He has left sufficient funds to see you through this pregnancy, and if you would need further allowances, he has informed me that you will receive them as quickly as the funds can be sent here. I am leaving some papers with you which tell you a bit about the Weingarten home. You should familiarize yourself with the routines of the home this afternoon. Dinner is served in the dining room at precisely 6 p.m., and one of the other girls on the floor can help you find your way there. I imagine that after your trip you will want to freshen up." Mrs. Kellogg looked her up and down. "Please see to it that you are on time and properly dressed this evening." She left the room, closing the door behind her.

Rose looked around before collapsing into one of the large sitting chairs. Properly dressed. She didn't even know what was in her suitcase.

She got up and walked over to the window nearest the twin bed. More maple trees blocked her view of what was on the other side of the tall white fence that separated the home from the next property. She walked over to the other window and found the view a little more open. She could see a bit of the downtown area of Winchester, but not enough to get a feel for much. She turned back to her comfortable prison, picked up her suitcase and placed it on the bed. She opened it, and on the very top was the yellow dress she had worn when she and Rafe had told their parents about the pregnancy. She picked up the dress and held it up to her body, remembering. Tears began to fill her eyes again…she couldn't even wear this dress now. Whoever had packed her suitcase certainly wasn't thinking about how her body was changing. Maybe her father had packed it himself, wanting to punctuate her heartbreak in his own cold, cruel way. That would be like him. The once-doting father had turned into a monster over the years. Rose thought again of her mother and how upset Daisy would be when she found out where Rose had been sent. She hoped her mother would come to see her, and that very thought made Rose realize she had already given up hope of getting out of this place. The tears spilled over.

Crying quietly, Rose unpacked her suitcase and put away her things. She took the chest of drawers and closet nearest the bed. When she saw the contents of her suitcase, she laughed bitterly. She had enough clothing to get through seven days – seven pairs of underpants, seven bras, seven pairs of socks as well as hosiery. Everything prepared in sevens. Lucky number seven.

There was no use to ruminate over such things. Finished with organizing her belongings, she sat back down in the chair nearest a window. She listened to a robin and watched as the bird fed its young in a nest sitting on a sheltered section of a sturdy branch. A Bible verse popped into her head. She didn't remember it exactly, but she recalled that it said something about even the littlest bird not falling to the ground without God knowing about it. She prayed that God knew she had fallen to the ground.

She drifted off, waking at 5 p.m. When she looked at the clock, she had a moment of panic, knowing she had but an hour to shower and 'dress properly.' She bolted out of the chair and began combing through her closet looking for something that fit well enough to wear to dinner. She pulled out a summer shift and jumped into the shower. She ran the water as hot as she could stand it on her skin, as if to scald off the grief she felt. Then she made herself as presentable as possible. She decided to wear no makeup or to curl her hair, leaving it straight and long.

As Rose walked out into the hall, several other girls were closing their doors behind them. A girl who looked to be nearly full-term approached her with a smile.

"Hello. My name is Alice D. I know you're new here. Can I help you find the dinner hall?" Alice did not have a Southern accent.

"Why, thank you, yes. I appreciate it very much. I'm Rose Caswell," Rose replied.

"Oh, gees, don't tell anyone your last name! You can only go by your last initial here." Alice looped her arm through Rose's and led her down the hall, back to the staircase Rose had ascended earlier. "The dining hall is on the first floor. The food is very good here, and nutritious, too. Your baby will have good nourishment." Alice smiled and they walked down the stairs. With her left hand, Alice held on to the stair railing.

"I had a fall a little earlier in my pregnancy, so I'm trying to be very careful," she said. "How far along are you?"

Rose was surprised at the openness with which Alice spoke of her pregnancy. She didn't know if she was prepared to reciprocate in such a forthright manner.

"I'm about four months now. It's been a pretty typical pregnancy as far as I can tell." She didn't really want to say much more than that.

Alice seemed to recognize that Rose was hesitant and changed the subject. "This place has a lot of rules. Have you read the rules yet? I'm thinking you haven't since you didn't know about the last name thing."

"No," replied Rose. "I fell asleep after I got unpacked. We left very early this morning and I felt pretty tired from the trip."

"Did you have far to come?" Alice inquired.

"Six hours. I'm from Kinston, North Carolina," Rose answered.

"That's a little bit of a trip, eh? Listen, just so you know, you better read the rules as soon as you can so that you don't unintentionally break any of them. Mrs. Kellogg is all business – there's no sympathy for not knowing the rules. Trust me, I found out the hard way."

Rose wondered about the 'hard way' Alice had learned this, but they were entering the dining hall. There were about twenty other girls there, already seated and looking a bit impatient with the last of the girls coming in.

"About time," said a girl who looked like she was all of fifteen. "We're starving."

"Oh, cool it, Deeny," Alice said. "It's just now six o'clock."

Mrs. Kellogg entered the room. All the girls were suddenly silent. Mrs. Kellogg approached the head of the table and remained standing. "Let's bow our heads."

Everyone did as commanded, though Rose kept her eyes open and tried to glance around.

"Father, for what we are about to receive, make us truly thankful. Amen." Mrs. Kellogg looked up while all the girls echoed "amen." Immediately, several older women entered the room carrying covered plates which were placed before each girl. No one removed their covers until everyone had been served. Then the lids came off and the room was filled with the noise of silverware clinking against china. There was no conversation, and Rose had the strong impression that conversation would not be welcomed at dinner. She ate in silence, as did the others. She noted that when a girl was done with her meal, she placed the lid back on her plate and sat quietly, her hands in her lap. The girls were almost robotic in this practice.

Mrs. Kellogg was the last to finish eating. When she was done, she announced, "You are all excused." Chairs were carefully pushed back and the girls began filing out, speaking quietly to each other as they made their way to the door.

"Miss Caswell, I trust you have made yourself comfortable in your room," Mrs. Kellogg said to Rose as she passed by.

"Yes, thank you," Rose said quietly, trying to move away from this unpleasant woman as quickly as possible.

"And you have brought yourself up to speed on our rules?" Mrs. Kellogg probed.

"No, not yet. I fell asleep. I intend to familiarize myself with them tonight," Rose replied.

"See to it that you do." Mrs. Kellogg turned her back to Rose.

Rose caught up with Alice. "I see what you mean about the rules. I better get reading."

"You'd be wise to do it tonight, for sure," Alice said. "She's a stickler. You're better off never getting on her bad side, I can tell you that. I have to confess that I'm glad it's almost time to have this baby and get out of here."

"At some point, you're going to have to tell me more about your experience, but for tonight, I better get myself buried in the rule book," Rose said as she stood at the door of her room. "Can we maybe go to breakfast together tomorrow?"

"You bet. Try to be ready at 7:45 sharp, ok? We'll walk down together again." Alice turned and started down the hallway to her own room. Then she turned and said, "Rose, you'll be ok here. It's scary at first. You don't know what to expect. But every one of us is in the same boat, and we all look out for each other. I promise – you'll be ok here."

Rose turned on the light in her room. The soft glow of evening came in through her window and she walked over to take it in. *This window will surely be my salvation*, she thought, appreciating her view of maple trees and forsythia.

She sat down and turned her attention to the rules Mrs. Kellogg had handed her this morning. It already felt like a long time had passed since she first entered this room.

The rule paper was simply a typed, numbered list of the home's expectations...or maybe just Mrs. Kellogg's expectations. Rose read with growing anxiety about what she was to endure before her baby was born, what all the girls who were here would endure.

'You are a resident of a premier home for unwed mothers, and you can be assured that you will receive only the finest medical care. You can also rest in the assurance that everything possible will be done to protect your privacy and the confidential nature of all aspects of your time here; that being the case, it is important that you not share your last name with others. The only people who should know your last name are members of the Weingarten staff.

It is important that you understand your responsibility to yourself, the unborn baby, and to the Weingarten home. Since this is a contract between you and the home, the following imperatives have been put into place.

1. **You will commit, in writing, to carrying your pregnancy to full term.**
2. **For the benefit of the baby, you will keep all physician appointments (3rd floor) and follow all recommendations of your physician.**
3. **You will participate in nutrition and exercise programs as directed by experts here at Weingarten.**

4. To address aberrant behaviors associated with your pregnancy, you will participate in psychological counseling.
5. You will participate in activities with other residents. These activities include, but are not limited to: educational classes (for those who have not completed high school), church services, chores.
6. Phone privileges are limited to parents (15 minutes; once a week only) and are granted after the first month of residency.
7. There will be no contact with males under any circumstances (other than your physician).
8. You may not leave the campus unescorted. Typical reasons for leaving the campus may be to shop for necessities or enjoy a group activity such as a movie.
9. As adoption offers the best opportunity to redeem your previous life and moves you forward to a productive and successful future, you will work with social workers to ensure a seamless adoption process.
10. Infraction of any of the stated rules may result in suspension of privileges. Repeated infraction may result in expulsion from the home without refund of tuition.'

Tuition? We're sure not in college, Rose thought. *No matter how clean and nice the surroundings, this is more like prison.* Without consciously realizing it, Rose had started considering how to make her escape.

8

When Rose didn't show up for school on Monday, Rafe didn't think that much about it. She had been having a lot of nausea, which seemed to be common among the pregnant women he had known all throughout his youth. He decided he would try calling her when he got home from school. The day crawled by slower than molasses.

He was scheduled to work at the newspaper office for a few hours that evening. Rafe was going home first to grab a bite to eat and call Rose before he left for the Daily Free Press.

When he arrived at the house, his mother was in the yard planting bulbs, making sure the yard was full of flowers for as many months in the year as they would bloom.

"Hey, son," Anne said. "How was your day today? Did you talk to Rose?"

"No, as a matter of fact, she wasn't even at school. I'm going to grab a sandwich and call her before I go over to the paper." He walked into the house, threw his books on the kitchen counter and began work on a sandwich. He dialed the Caswell's number. As he spread peanut butter on bread, he held the phone between his chin and his shoulder and waited for someone to pick up on the other end.

"Caswell residence," a voice said.

"Miss Stella, good afternoon. Is Rose available?"

After too long a period of silence, Rafe heard Miss Stella's voice, shaky and uncertain.

"Mr. Rafe, Miss Rose ain't here. She's just not here. I have to go."

"Miss Stella, wait…." It was too late. Rafe heard the receiver click down on its base. His hands began to tremble.

Anne had walked into the kitchen and crossed to the sink to wash her hands as Rafe stood silently at the counter. He was pale and tense. "What's wrong son? You look like someone just died."

"Something very bad is going on, Mom. I just called the Caswell place. Miss Stella answered the phone and said Rose isn't there. She hung up fast, like she was scared to even talk to me. I have a really bad feeling about this. You know I told you Ham was furious about Rose being pregnant. Well what I didn't tell you was that he knocked Rose right down on the floor. I'm scared for her. I'm going to call the paper and let them know I won't be there. I'm going over to the Caswell's."

"Son, it's time for your father and I to be a part of this. Let's wait for him to get home. He and Ham were friends all those years ago in high school…maybe your dad can talk some sense into him," Anne offered. "Let's wait till Dad gets home."

"Ok. I'm sure you're right and I appreciate your help, but I'm really worried now. I can't eat this," Rafe said, throwing his half-made sandwich into the trash.

"Worrying won't help, but praying might," Anne said. "Why don't you do that?" She smiled and gave Rafe a little hug. "We're going to get through this, son. You'll see."

Rafe called his boss, Jim Fussell, and told him he wouldn't be at work. "I can't explain tonight, Jim. Just please trust me on this, and forgive me calling off at the last minute." Jim must have heard the worry in his voice because he said, "Don't give it another thought, Rafe. We'll talk when you're here on Wednesday." Rafe felt relieved by Jim's understanding, but dreaded having to tell him this whole story.

He tried to concentrate on the little homework he had, but concentration came hard.

His dad got home right on time. Rafe went downstairs, but Anne was already in the process of letting his dad know what had happened. Glenn sat down at the kitchen table.

"Darling, can you pour me a Coca Cola and let me think about how to approach this before we go rushing out there," Glenn said. Anne went to the refrigerator and returned with the soda pop.

"Rafe, it may not be as ominous as it sounds, so let's make sure we have our heads on straight before we head out there. Give me a minute…." Glenn took a long sip of Coke and looked up at the ceiling. Several minutes passed in silence, while Rafe drummed his fingers on the table. Suddenly Glenn said, "Let's go."

"Wait, Dad, what's the plan? What am I supposed to do?" Rafe was a little frantic.

"Nothing son. Let me do the talking. Mom can sit with Daisy and hand-hold her through this discussion. You and I will stand side-by-side, but I'll do the talking, ok?" Glenn seemed very confident.

"Ok. I wish you'd let me in on it, though." Rafe and Anne followed Glenn to the car, Anne linking her arm through Rafe's.

"We're just going to have an honest, friendly talk," Glenn answered over his shoulder.

It was a quiet ride out to the Caswell's. Anne stared out the passenger side window; Rafe kept his eyes on his parents. He noticed that his father's jaw clenched and unclenched, then clenched again. He knew his father was nervous, though he would never admit that.

"It's the dinner hour...not a good time to go knocking on peoples' doors," Glenn said, "but it's one way of hedging your bet that they will actually be at home."

They arrived at the big house, parked and walked up the long set of steps to the porch. Glenn rang the doorbell. It took a minute before anyone answered.

"They probably can't believe anyone would be rude enough to show up here at this hour," Glenn chuckled.

The door opened, and Miss Stella stood staring at them with her mouth slightly open.

"Good evening, Miss Stella," Rafe said. "Have you ever met my parents?"

"Mr. Rafe, you hadn't oughta be here tonight," Miss Stella said, her voice quavering.

"Stella, you remember me...I'm Anne." Rafe's mother stepped forward and offered Stella a handshake. Stella took Anne's hand and gave a weak smile.

"Of course, Miz Whitfield, I remember you. Beggin' your pardon if I seem rude, but this is not a good day to be here."

"We know this is a difficult time, but it's vital that we see Mr. and Mrs. Caswell this evening. It's a matter of great importance." Anne spoke gently and calmly. Stella still looked uneasy.

"Well, I'll tell the family you're here."

Stella disappeared down the hall to the dining room. She had said "the family."

"Maybe I was worried for nothing. Maybe Rose just wasn't here when I called." Rafe was trying to convince himself as much as anyone.

"Perhaps, son." Glenn stepped forward a little further into the house. It had been a long time since Glenn had been inside the Caswell mansion, but not a lot had changed since he and Ham played football together. Ham's mother had always invited the team over at the end of football season for a party, whether the team had done well or not. The memory made him comfortable in these surroundings, though the discussion to come would likely be anything *but* comfortable.

Hamilton Caswell appeared in the hall. His purposeful stride was intended to intimidate. He was ready for the Whitfield family. He did not offer his hand to Glenn.

"Good evening, Ham, and pardon the intrusion, but we wanted to talk to you about Rose and Rafe," Glenn started. "Can we sit down somewhere and talk for a little bit?"

Daisy had appeared in the doorway of the dining room, and Stuart had joined the group. He casually leaned up against the wall and surveyed the Whitfields with half a smile on his face. He was going to enjoy the fireworks.

Ham led the Whitfields into the sitting room and pointed to seats. He still had not said a word. Daisy followed Ham and stood behind his chair. Stu resumed his relaxed stance along a wall.

"We've known each other a very long time," Glenn said, "I'd like for us to be able to talk about this situation man-to-man or family-to-family, since it affects everyone."

"What situation are you referring to?" Ham answered. "The situation where my daughter's life has been all but ruined? The situation where my family's name had been plopped into the pigsty?"

"Now Ham, I know this is not how we would have wanted our kids to start their adult lives, but it has happened and now we have to deal with it in the most appropriate way," Glenn countered. "Rafe is sorry and I'm sure Rose is just as sorry that they have gotten themselves into this situation, but as parents, I think our challenge is to help them pull their behinds out of the fire and get them on the road to a stable life together."

"Don't presume to tell me what my 'challenge' is," Ham seethed, "and don't bother to tell me how sorry Rafe is. It's not hard to figure what he sniffed around Rose for."

"What the heck do you mean by that?" Rafe stood up and took a step towards the man.

Ham glowered at Rafe, a look so intimidating Rafe took a small step back. "Just exactly what it sounded like. All you were ever interested in was the inheritance Rose will receive when I'm in the ground." Rafe was dumbfounded. Rose's inheritance was truly the last thing he had ever thought of. If anything, he wanted to free her from the burden of the family name and their oppressive wealth, wealth that choked the creativity and joy right out of everyone in their family. Hamilton was a manipulative, power-hungry bully. Daisy was a spineless, quivering afterthought to Ham. Stuart was a drunk. Only Rose seemed to have escaped the family's dysfunction, but she was still vulnerable.

Rafe tried to maintain control of his voice. "Sir, I'm not one bit interested in your money and never was. I love Rose. That's why I've been hanging around for the last year. I don't want your money. I'll earn my own."

"By being a *journalist?*" Hamilton's tone was derisive, mocking.

"Ham, journalists make a decent living." Glenn now stepped in again. "Rafe's not interested in your business, just as he's not interested in my business...."

Hamilton cut him off. "Your business? Why would he be interested in that when he can forego work at all and inherit my money? Your business? Grease monkey?" Hamilton laughed, and it was a bitter sound.

"Seems my line of work has been good enough for you all these years of fixing your vehicles. Let's get back to the matter at hand," Glenn answered in a solemn tone.

"There's no discussion to be had," Hamilton answered. "My daughter will not be marrying your son. She has left the county and will not be returning for some time. This was the choice she made after she came to her senses."

Stuart was enjoying the looks on the Whitfield family faces. All three of them had their mouths hanging wide open.

"I don't believe you," Rafe began. "Rose loves me and I know it. She wanted to marry me. We talked about it together many times before all this happened. I don't believe she would leave me willingly."

"What are you implying, boy?" Ham replied. "Who do you think you are to come into my home uninvited and unannounced and call me a liar? I told you Rose left of her own accord. You'll not marry her now or ever."

"What about the baby?" Anne now spoke up. "What about your *grandchild*?" she asked, putting emphasis on the word that might remind Ham that this baby was going to be his progeny, too.

"That's nothing you need to worry about," Ham said menacingly. Anne saw Daisy wince at this pronouncement. She stood up and walked over to Daisy, putting her arm around Daisy's shoulders.

"Daisy, wouldn't we make the best, most loving grandmothers?" Anne asked her, but she could see the fear in Daisy's wide eyes. Daisy was not about to affirm any such declaration.

"Ham, I'm appealing to your higher nature, now. Can't you see beyond your 'family name' for a minute and think about the beautiful child your daughter is going to bring into the world? Rafe wants to help shoulder the responsibility and be a good father to that child. You're not giving these kids a chance. They're both good kids who made a dumb mistake, but one they own up to and want to make as right as possible." Glenn tried the powers of persuasion that had helped him stay on Ham's good side when they were teenagers themselves.

Hamilton stood up and walked to where Daisy and Anne stood together. Anne removed her arm from Daisy's shoulders and moved a little closer to Glenn. Ham looked hard at Daisy, then turned to face Glenn.

"There is no making this 'right.' Even if I were inclined to change my mind, which I am not, Rose would not change *her* mind. There will be no marriage between these two children, now or ever. As for the lot of you, you may leave my house. I don't expect to ever have another discussion like this with any of you. Stay off my property; stay away from my family. Your son has done enough damage for a lifetime…keep away from the Caswells." He grabbed Daisy's arm and walked from the sitting room into the hall, turning only to add, "And if you ever talk about this to anyone, if you ever show up here again, my lawyers will take your grease monkey business right down to the ground."

"Ham, you should know me well enough to know that I don't care much for threats," Glenn replied.

"It is not a threat," Ham responded. "It's a promise." He continued down the hall, leaving the Whitfields in the sitting room with Stuart.

"Y'all have a good evening," Stuart smirked as he left the room.

All three Whitfields stood, looked at each other, and headed out into the hall to leave. Miss Stella was at the front door with her hand on the doorknob, waiting to let them out.

"Good-bye, Miss Stella," Glenn said to her, but she looked only at Rafe. Rafe knew she was on the verge of tears, and he gave her the littlest kiss on the cheek.

"Good-bye, Mr. Rafe," she said. "You're a good boy." Rafe knew she meant it.

The dejected family walked to the car and got in. Rafe became animated as soon as the doors closed.

"What are we going to do, Dad? We can't let him get away with this. He's forced Rose to leave, I know that. And he's openly threatened you. We can't let him push us around like this."

Glenn started the car and headed down the driveway. "Son, I'm not sure what the next move is. I think we better take a little time to consider what is best all the way around." He looked over at Anne, who was sitting with her eyes closed. Glenn knew she was probably praying.

"Well, I already know what I'm going to do," Rafe said. "I'm going to find Rose. I'm going to find Rose and marry her."

9

That very same Monday morning, Rose was awakened by the Virginia sun shining in her window. She looked at her watch. 6:30 a.m. – enough time to make herself presentable for breakfast. As she showered, she looked forward to meeting up with Alice and hoped they'd have a chance to talk. Rose needed to know more about the Weingarten home and particularly, Mrs. Kellogg.

She was in the hall outside her room at 7:55 – she had missed Alice, but she knew where the dining hall was now, so she didn't have to wait for someone to direct her. She flew down the long staircase and entered the dining room. Alice was already at the table, and she waved to Rose – she had saved a seat for her.

"Good morning. How was your first night? I was a little worried when I didn't see you at 7:45," Alice greeted her.

"Fine, actually. Sorry I was late…I slept really well. I read all the rules of this place last night and thought I'd have nightmares, but I didn't," Rose told her, unfolding her napkin on her lap.

"All that stuff puts you off at first. It sounds so…unyielding. But honestly, once you get a feel of the place, it's not bad. Mrs. Kellogg is the tough nut to crack around here, but if you stick by those rules, you'll be fine," Alice reminded her.

Once again, the all-female wait staff served breakfast, wholesome and delicious. Rose could have gladly eaten more, but it was clear that the nutritional guidelines that had been discussed in the rules included limitations on calories. Mrs. Kellogg was not present for breakfast, so the room was filled with the sound of young women talking and laughing. Rose marveled at the difference between now and last evening.

After breakfast, Rose and Alice walked back up to their rooms. Rose found a paper hanging on her door. She pulled it off and discovered an itinerary for her first day at Cordelia Weingarten.

"Are you kidding me? We have a schedule?" Rose was incredulous.

"Oh my heavens, yes. We're kept busy from sun up to sun down around here. You won't enjoy a lot of free time." Alice's voice had taken on a little bit of a sarcastic tone. "It's part of your penance. What's the first thing on your list?"

"I have to be in the doctor's office at 9:00, be in the psychologist's office at 9:30, meet with the social worker at 10:00, meet with Mrs. Kellogg at 11:00, lunch at noon. Then in the afternoon, it looks like just exercise and chores. It doesn't say what my chores are."

Alice smiled. "Oh, you'll find out from Mrs. Kellogg, I guarantee it."

"Ok. I'll look forward to that. I'm probably going to have to clean toilets or something since I'm the new girl," Rose said.

"You never know with Mrs. Kellogg. I'll see you later." Alice headed for her own room.

It was 8:45. Rose had a few minutes to brush her teeth and go to the bathroom before she had to see the physician. In the bathroom mirror, she noticed circles under her eyes. She didn't remember ever seeing them before. She thought she might mention it to the doctor.

There was an elevator available from the second to the third floor, but it was marked TO LABOR AND DELIVERY ROOMS ONLY, so she walked the steps. The third floor appeared deserted at first, but she soon saw a nurse in a crisply starched white uniform carrying a clipboard out of one of the rooms, all of which had closed doors. She followed the nurse to a station where the nurse sat down.

"How may I help you?" the nurse asked.

"I'm Rose Caswell, and I'm supposed to see the doctor at 9:00," Rose said.

"I'm happy to meet you Rose," the nurse smiled. "I'm Nurse White, but that feels pretty formal so I ask all the girls to just call me Deb."

"Thank you so much." This woman's disposition made Rose feel more at ease than she had at any time since she arrived. "Is there someplace I am supposed to wait?"

"Actually, I'll take you right into one of the exam rooms. You can get ready for your exam. I guess you know you'll have to have a pelvic exam today since this is your first appointment with us. Once you've had your exam, I'll tell you a little about how things run around here."

Deb accompanied Rose to an exam room. A paper-covered exam table with stirrups, a small cupboard, and some instruments on a metal stand were all that the room contained. It was cold. Rose dreaded having to undress. She had already had a pelvic exam, so she knew what to expect. She hated the idea.

"Here's a gown to put on. You should remove your slacks and underpants. You don't need to take your blouse off," Deb explained. "Then just sit here on the end of the table and I'll come back with Dr. Oppenheimer. He cares for all the girls here."

Rose did as she was told. She was glad for one smiling face among those who were in positions of authority. She hoped Dr. Oppenheimer would be the same.

He was not. He was quiet, professional, and distant, but appeared to be competent.

"You have a very normal pregnancy going on here. It will be important for you to eat right – not gain too much weight – exercise every day, and get adequate rest," Dr. Oppenheimer told her while he wrote on his clipboard. He never looked at her face one time. "Nurse White will get your baseline weight and height, as well as check your blood pressure and so forth." He left the room. She had forgotten to mention the circles under her eyes.

Deb had stayed at his side during the exam, and now she spoke up. "Rose, he might seem kind of cold, but he's a very good doctor. That's the truth. I've seen his work for many years now. He will do a great job taking care of you. He just doesn't get too involved like maybe your family doctor would. How's about stepping over here to the scale?"

Rose got on the scale and found that she had gained only a few pounds. "Nurse White, I've only gained 3 pounds. Is that normal? Shouldn't I be gaining more than that?" she asked.

Deb laughed. "Ok, first of all stop calling me Nurse White – I'm Deb, remember? Then, don't worry about not gaining more weight. That will come later. By that time, you'll be asking us if we're sure the scale isn't out of order. Trust me on that."

Deb checked her blood pressure and pulse. "Everything seems to be fine. Do you think you can pee? I need to do a urine test on you."

"Well, I went to the bathroom right before I came up here, but I can try," Rose said.

"Great. Take this little bottle into the bathroom at the end of the hall. When you get some urine in there, close it up tight, put the whole thing in this little plastic bag, and bring it to me. I'll be at the nurse's station, ok?"

She had noticed more frequent urination since she was a little farther along, so Rose had no trouble providing a specimen. She packaged it up as instructed and took it to the nurse's station.

"Thanks, Rose. Now you won't have to come back for a month unless you have some kind of problem. If so, make sure you let us know about it right away. If I'm not here, my co-worker, Angie Sweeney will be here. One of us is always here. There are a couple of other nurses who work here, too - mostly in the delivery area - but Angie and I will be seeing you prior to having the baby," Deb told her.

"How do I get hold of you?" Rose asked.

"You can just come up the steps and we'll either find some time for you or we'll book an appointment if it's not some kind of immediate need – in other words, an emergency," Deb replied.

"And if there's an emergency?" Rose inquired.

"Get one of the other girls or Mrs. Kellogg to run up and get us…then we'll come down to your room and do our initial examination there," Deb explained. "We have had to send a couple of girls to the hospital in the past. Our delivery room is really intended for only the uncomplicated pregnancy, and 99% of the time, they are."

"Ok. You've been more than kind, and I thank you. What time next month?"

Deb handed her a small card with a day and time on it. Rose thought she would start a calendar for her appointments. Then she could keep track of all her other activities, too. She didn't want to land on Mrs. Kellogg's bad side because of not maintaining the schedule she was supposed to follow. At least, that was, until she could get out of there.

The psychologist's office was on the first floor, very near Mrs. Kellogg's office. WILTON PICKENS, PhD, the nameplate on the door said. She knocked and heard a voice from within. "Come in."

Rose opened the door tentatively and peeked around it. She saw a thin, balding man with an unlit pipe in his mouth. He wore a worn-looking tweed suit with patches on the elbows, giving what Rose thought might be the stereotypical appearance of a college professor.

"Well, what are you waiting for? I do not bark; nor do I bite," Dr. Pickens said. His voice was cold.

"I'm sorry. I don't mean to be rude," Rose said. "I just wanted to make sure I wasn't intruding...."

"How silly," he interrupted, settling himself into his office chair. "I would not have invited you in if you were an intrusion. Please sit down, miss." Dr. Pickens pointed to a chair across the desk from him. Rose walked over and sat down, trying to withdraw into the chair as best she could. This man was as intimidating as Mrs. Kellogg.

"Do you know how you got pregnant? What I mean is, do you understand the process that leads to pregnancy?" Dr. Pickens looked at her over the top of his wire-rimmed glasses.

Rose shifted uncomfortably in the chair. "Well, yes, of course," she stammered.

"I only ask because, first of all, I have to make sure that you have knowledge of how pregnancy is a result of the act of having sex and that you understand right from wrong. Obviously, sex outside of marriage is wrong. My job here is to help young women such as yourself overcome their immoral or deviant behaviors as they relate to sex. I can't do that if you don't understand the process in the first place."

Rose could feel her cheeks burning. She glared at the repugnant man in front of her and tried without much success to maintain a neutral face. "Of course I know about sex."

"Well, young lady, you'd be surprised at how many girls do *not* have that knowledge. You'd be surprised at how many girls are victims of incest, and you'd be surprised at how many girls are simply wanton in their ways – nymphomaniacs, really – without an understanding of the consequences. You're fortunate in that you are a step ahead of many of the girls who are currently in residence here." Dr. Pickens lit his pipe. "Let's start in your childhood. How is your relationship with your mother and father?"

Rose didn't know what to say. This was the crudest conversation she had been part of since her father threw Rafe out of the house.

"Dr. Pickens, my relationship with my mother and father is fine. My father is certainly a controlling man, or I wouldn't be sitting before you right now. However, I love both of my parents. I also love the man who is the father of this baby I'm carrying. Unfortunately, my father didn't love him; that's the reason I'm here."

"Are you sure of all that? About the father of the baby, I mean." Dr. Pickens had leaned across his desk slightly.

"Absolutely. Yes, I'm sure. My boyfriend asked me to marry him but my father threw him out. We would have been married already if it was up to us," Rose stated. "My father has schemed all of this up." Rose waved her hand through the air. "All this − the home, the separation from my family − this is all his work."

"Well, then, it sounds as if your relationship with your father is not exactly what you first stated," Dr. Pickens smirked.

"Until this time, I have understood my father and respected him. Right now, we're on the outs, no doubt about it, but it doesn't make me love him less. I'm frustrated with his sending me off like a thief in the night, but I'll be speaking with him and I'm sure he'll change his mind with a little more time." Rose was trying to sound more confident than she really was.

Dr. Pickens picked up a file, leafed through a few pages, then said to Rose, "Well, we will surely see about that. In the meantime, I'd like to see you next week on Thursday at 10 a.m. We will need to dig into the feelings that brought you to participate in sex outside of marriage and deal with the corresponding behaviors. You do not want to end up in a situation like this again, I assume."

"Good day, sir." Rose was angry and had nothing else to offer. She stood up and left the room as quickly as she could.

She had a couple of minutes before she was due in the social worker's office, and that was a good thing. She took a few deep breaths and tried to calm herself. Why was it that if a girl had sex it was a 'deviant behavior' but it was almost an expectation of boys? Why were girls whisked off to homes like this while boys went on with their normal lives? She had not been so angry since her father...*don't think about it now.*

The social worker's office was down the hall closer to the dining room. If the social worker was anything like the psychologist, Rose thought she would come undone. She knocked on the door and heard a voice call, "Come in." This time, she opened the door and stepped inside without hesitation. A young woman was putting some manila folders into a filing cabinet. She turned to look at Rose. "You must be our new girl, Miss Caswell. Please come over and have a seat."

Rose found a comfortable chair and sat down while the social worker finished what she was doing. Rose thought she moved like someone with a lot of nervous energy – quick, jerky, but at the same time, precise and ordered.

"I'm Kathryn Baker. I'm the social worker here. I have been at Cordelia Weingarten for the last six years," she began.

"Golly, you look awfully young to have been here six years," Rose replied.

Kathryn smiled. "Well, thanks, but yes, I've been doing this for a while now. I've got a lot of experience under my belt because about 100 girls a year go through here. I've been responsible for arranging adoptions for each of those young ladies and with few exceptions, we've accomplished a satisfactory arrangement for every one of them. I have a Master's degree in social work, and this has become my specialty. Now tell me about yourself."

Rose hesitated, thrown off for a second by the mention of adoption. How could she begin her story and help this woman understand her intent to keep her child? "Well, I'm 18. I'm about four months pregnant. My boyfriend and I wanted to get married but were prevented from doing so by my father. He's the one who sent me here. I've read all the rules of this place. I've met the physician and the psychologist, and now you. I've only met one other girl so far. Frankly, I'd already like to leave." She was surprised at her own bluntness.

"Well, thank you for being honest, at least. Let's spend a little time talking about why it's important for you to stay and why it's important for you to be focused on adoption, shall we?" Kathryn Baker did not seem to be giving her much of a choice as she continued without waiting for Rose to respond.

"Very often the girls who come here have a feeling they could parent their child. As you have already surely seen, the girls who are here are all young. You all have had little experience with small children and are ill-prepared for the responsibilities of parenting. I mean no disrespect in those statements. Some of the girls who are here cared for younger brothers and sisters, but even then, they do not have the same level of responsibility as a parent who must provide for all the child's needs. Single parenting, particularly, does not fall in line with the natural order of things. Additionally, think about your future. Would you want to be raising a child alone with your reputation sullied? Could you provide for an illegitimate child on your own? Do you think you would ever be able to find a husband who would accept an illegitimate child?" She paused.

Rose was shocked by the diatribe. She recognized this as an attempt to brainwash her.

"First of all, I would not be single," Rose began. "My boyfriend and I had every intention of getting married. We love each other very much."

"Then where is he?" Kathryn said. "Would he really allow you to languish here if he was intent on marrying you? Wouldn't he be pounding on the front door trying to get you out of here?" The social worker revealed a cynical smile.

"I'm sure he doesn't even know where I am. My father will keep us apart unless I can convince him otherwise," Rose said.

"It's highly unlikely that your father will change his mind, based on what I know. He has already paid for your stay here in its entirety. That indicates only one thing…he means for you to stay here until you deliver the baby, at which time, the baby will be given to waiting parents."

Rose sat quietly, once again feeling the cold grip of fear on her heart.

"You understand that there are hundreds of families who wish for a child and do not have the ability to have one of their own? Those families' hearts are breaking for a child. Your baby, while conceived under less than ideal circumstances, can fill out that family circle for some man and woman. You have an obligation to do what is right for this baby," Kathryn continued. "Even if you managed to get out of here, how would you care for yourself? Could you afford the type of medical care available to you here? Would you have such a nice place to stay? Would you have the type of friendships and support you will develop here? What kind of work skills do you have? Could you even get a job? There's a lot to think about, Rose."

Rose stood up. She felt as though she were carrying a heavy weight and could barely move. "I must go lie down," she said.

"Of course, of course. But think about the things we've talked about this morning, and I'll come to visit you next week." Kathryn walked to the door and opened it for Rose. "Think about our discussion, Rose."

Rose headed for the staircase, and just as she put her foot on the first step, the door to Mrs. Kellogg's office opened, and she stepped out. "Miss Caswell, were you forgetting that you need to see me?"

Rose stopped. "I don't feel very well. Could we meet a little later?"

Mrs. Kellogg snorted. "No, we could not. There are more girls here than just you, you know. My schedule is very strict."

Rose stepped back down and walked to Mrs. Kellogg's office. Mrs. Kellogg closed the door behind them and said, "Our conversation need not take too long. You don't even need to sit down unless you want to. I just wanted to make sure you read the rules of the house and that you understand how important your compliance with those rules will be."

Rose was starting to feel dizzy and weak, but she muttered, "Yes," and Mrs. Kellogg continued.

"Your father has given us instructions about his expectations for your time here, and they fall right in line with my philosophy about how to deal with unwed mothers. He has generously paid in advance for your entire stay and has asked us to maintain a private room for you. You may not know that private rooms are not generally allowed. He has also informed us that you have been insistent upon marrying the boy who fathered your child. You must know by now that such a thing will not happen. Your father is protecting your future, and for that, you should be grateful. If you aren't now, you will be someday. I expect that you will abide by all the rules, that you will follow all physician instructions, that you will sign the adoption papers at the appropriate time...." She stopped talking for a second and looked closer at Rose's face. "Are you quite all right?"

"I don't feel...." Rose started to say, but the floor came up and stopped her from saying anything else.

* * *

When she came to, she was in her room lying on her bed. Deb White was sitting in a chair next to her.

"Hey, how are you feeling?" Deb's kind eyes reminded Rose of Miss Stella in many ways – compassionate and caring.

"I'm all right, I think. My head hurts a little bit. I don't remember exactly what happened," Rose said, starting to sit up.

"Hold on there, let me help you. I'll tell you what happened," Deb said as she assisted Rose to a sitting position on the side of the bed. "You passed out and hit the deck. You're lucky you didn't crack your noggin. Mrs. Kellogg saw you were going down and kind of prevented you from falling flat on your face."

"Oh, yes…Mrs. Kellogg. Well, I guess I should be grateful to her for that, at least. As I recall, she was giving me a lecture at the time," Rose said. "I'll probably get another one for rudely passing out while she was talking."

Deb sat back down in the chair directly across from Rose, grabbed both of her hands, and looked Rose right in the eyes.

"Rose, my job here is to help the physician keep you healthy so that you deliver a healthy baby. It's not my place to tell you what to do…only to help keep you healthy. I'm not a shrink, I'm not a social worker, but I am a human being and a nurse, and I must give you this one piece of advice. You're in a no-win situation. There are a lot of girls here who are in even *more* of a no-win situation than you. At least you have parents who care about you and are providing a decent environment for you. Some of the girls don't even have that. Yes, Mrs. Kellogg is tough, and so are some of the other folks here. They cut themselves off emotionally so they won't carry the hurt and sorrow that often comes to stay here with these girls." She rolled her eyes. "At least I *think* that's why they are the way they are. Anyway, try to make friends with some of the other girls here. Don't let Mrs. Kellogg or the others stress you out. Keep your head down, do what you are supposed to do. Your pregnancy is going to go by very quickly and you'll be back out of here, getting on with your life. It's the only way, really. We're just not living in a time that accepts your situation very well. I suspect that someday women will decide to keep their babies more, maybe even have babies without husbands on purpose, but we're just not in that time right now." She sat back in her chair, releasing her grip on Rose's hands. "You can make it through this and come out better on the other side."

Rose sat quietly for a minute, then said, "I'm so very sad. My boyfriend and I wanted to get married. Not only are we not getting married, I'm being forced to give away our child. How can I possibly 'come out better on the other side'?" she questioned.

Deb rose and walked towards the door. "It stinks. It really does. But you must hold on to hope, Rose. Otherwise, you'll never get through this. She smiled. "I'll see you next month as we planned, but if you need me, just holler, ok?" She closed the door behind her, leaving Rose sitting alone with her thoughts.

10

Graduation came and went. Rafe went through the motions, barely passing his final exams. All his friends knew something was terribly wrong, but Rafe always told them he was fine and was just having a hard time deciding what to do about college. A few people asked him about Rose, but he told them that they had broken up. He didn't know what else to say for now. He knew people whispered about where Rose might be, and he assumed people had figured out that she had been sent away because of pregnancy. That was what typically happened to unwed mothers…they were sent away to an aunt or a sister, usually disappearing suddenly.

He was despondent. He loved Rose so much, yet had no idea of how to find her. He was convinced that she loved him and that she never would have left willingly. He had to become a detective, had to break through the Caswell stonewall.

It occurred to him that Miss Stella might be his link to the truth, to information about where Rose might be. She appeared to be a timid little woman, but she definitely had her ear to the ground at the Caswell place. She knew what was going on at all times. Rafe decided that somehow, he would get time alone with her and press her for any details she might know. Rafe knew Miss Stella liked him and he felt bad taking advantage of that affection, but he knew of no other way.

There was only one grocery store in Kinston and Rafe knew Miss Stella did the shopping for the kitchen provisions. He didn't know the shopping schedule, so he started visiting the ice cream stand across the street from the store on a more regular basis, watching and waiting for her to appear. He tried different days, different times, knowing it would be nothing but pure luck if he actually made contact with her.

Finally, luck was on his side. On a Tuesday morning, Rafe saw Miss Stella park an old green Chrysler and head for the front door of the Piggly Wiggly. He sprinted across the street, calling her name. Miss Stella looked up and around, trying to locate the familiar voice calling her.

"Miss Stella," Rafe said as he got within a few feet. "Please don't go in the store yet. I've got to talk to you. Let's go have a Coke across the street."

"Now, Mr. Rafe, you know what would happen to me if any of them Caswells saw me talkin' to you. I'd lose my job, boy." Miss Stella was not as nervous as she had been at the house when Rafe last saw her, but she was still cautious.

"Miss Stella, I'm begging you. You know I love Rose. I have to find her."

Stella looked at him, turned and took a few steps towards the store, then stopped and spun back around to look at Rafe. "Son, I know you love that girl and so do I. She ain't happy where she been sent, I can tell you that. I overheard Mr. Ham tellin' Miz Daisy 'bout the whole thing. Rose's daddy done packed her up and drove her off to the city of Chicago. He got a sister up yonder who Miss Rose will stay with till she have that baby of your'n. Now you don't never tell no one that you got this information from me. If you do, I will put my hand right on the Bible – on the very word of God – and swear you tellin' a lie. You understand me?"

"Yes, Miss Stella, I do," Rafe said, "but where in Chicago is Rose? Do you know the address or anything that would help me find her? Chicago is a big city."

Miss Stella looked puzzled for a minute, then said, "Mr. Rafe, I don't reckon I done you one bit of help. I don't know where in Chicago Mr. Ham's sister lives." She looked crestfallen, as if she had failed and knew it.

"Don't worry, Miss Stella," Rafe said. "You've been good to me always, and I appreciate that you put your job on the line to even talk to me. Don't worry about Rose or me. I intend to find her if I have to walk down every street in Chicago."

"Well, I wish you the very best on that. You always been my favorite gentleman friend Miss Rose ever brought home." Stella lowered her eyes, and Rafe thought she might have blushed.

"And you've always been as kind to me as a human can be when they're not related," Rafe smiled at Miss Stella. "I will always appreciate your kindness and friendship."

Miss Stella blushed again and said, "You take care now, boy. Don't come around the Caswells, don't let no one know what you're up to. You take care...." She trailed off, turned and walked into the Piggly Wiggly.

Chicago. Only about a thousand miles. Only about a sixteen hour drive. Only half-way across the United States. Only God knows how many miles of streets to cover with no address to refer to. Despite how overwhelmed he felt, Rafe immediately developed a new sense of determination....

11

Day-to-day life with twenty or so other pregnant girls can be like a roller coaster ride, Rose decided. Throughout the month of June, she tried to learn more about her inmates, as she called them in her mind. She had tried to make friends, but for the most part, people were stand-offish, private, each person absorbed in what was happening to them and their bodies.

Alice continued to be the person Rose was closest to, and even Alice kept a bit of distance between them. They walked around the grounds behind the home one afternoon, and Rose tried to get to know her better.

"Alice, when exactly are you due?" Rose asked.

"Middle-to-late September. What about you?" Alice replied.

Rose thought for just a second. "Sometime in November...I'm guessing about the middle of November. I got pregnant in February. We didn't tell our parents till the end of May and of course, I ended up here soon after." She paused, remembering back. "My father was so angry at us. How did your parents take the news?"

Alice walked over to a bench under a tree and sat down. "Well, my mother has been dead since I was thirteen. It was just me, my brother, and my dad for so long. When I told my dad I was pregnant, he started crying. He blamed it on himself. He said that without our mom, he was responsible; he was supposed to protect me from the world, and he felt he had failed. It was pitiful. I couldn't have felt worse about it. It wasn't anyone's fault but my own, of course."

"What about the baby's father?" Rose asked. "Has he been involved at all? I mean, did he want the baby? Did you guys want to get married?"

"Oh heavens no! We were just hormonal, had sex, and got into this mess." Alice smiled. "Kid stuff, you know?"

"Gosh, I don't think I would ever even consider having sex unless I was in love," Rose said. "That's the problem for me. I love my boyfriend, Rafe, and he loves me, and here we are, worlds apart thanks to my father. I'm sure Rafe doesn't have a clue where I am. I know that if he did, he'd have been here by now."

"Rose, how sure are you about that? I'm not trying to be mean, but I think boys sometimes tell girls they love them when they really just want to have sex. They might like the girl, but what they really *love* is sex. Do you know what I mean?" Alice didn't want to hurt Rose, but she definitely had a different perspective on the whole subject. "I hope you know I mean no offense."

"First, I'm not offended, and second, I'm very sure. If there's one thing I've seen, it's how love is demonstrated," Rose began. "I've seen love at its best and at its worst. My parents are examples of the latter. How two people could stay married to each other when they clearly have no use for each other is a mystery to me. My father can be mean as a rattlesnake, especially to my mother. My mother just takes it, and I think it's because she doesn't think she has any other option. It's sad. On the other hand, Rafe's mom and dad are really in love, even after being married for so many years. They respect each other, talk to each other, are openly affectionate, holding hands and all that kind of stuff. It's a simple demonstration, but to me, Rafe's parents are what marital love should look like."

"My mom wasn't alive long enough for me to really see that in my parents. As far as I could tell my dad never even looked at another woman after my mom died. That said, I don't know that I've seen that kind of relationship in any other adults I knew. I'm not kidding. Maybe I just didn't pay attention," Alice said.

"Well, when you see it, you appreciate it, that's for sure, especially when you are comparing it to what I've seen in *my* parents. I wonder sometimes how my mother has lived through it. And we have never known what to do about my father's abuse. Alice, he has hit her so hard he left bruises sometimes." Rose looked down at her hands. "I can't help but love my father and have an appreciation of the life he has built, but he is brutal to my mother, and I loathe that behavior."

"Gees, can't the cops do something about the beating?" Alice was aghast.

"Mother would never even think to press charges against him," Rose said. "My belief is that she thinks so little of herself that she probably blames herself for it. It's sad and hard to fathom."

"Well, if any man ever hit me, it would be the *last* time he hit me," Alice avowed. "I'd never tolerate someone beating me."

"Alice, where are you from?" Rose asked.

"I don't think we're supposed to tell each other that kind of stuff," started Alice, "but what the heck? I'm from New Jersey."

"New Jersey! How in the world did you ever get down here?" Rose was surprised at the distance Alice had come.

"It wasn't that hard, really. You just have to make the right connections to find out where you can go when you're in this boat. Then you have to come up with the money. My dad helped me, he felt so bad about me 'not knowing about sex,' or so he thought. He brought me down and he'll pick me up when the baby has been born."

Rose was quiet for a minute. "I got dropped off here by our driver. I have no idea who's coming for me when this is all over."

"You have a driver!" Alice's eyes were wide. "Your family must be loaded! Must be nice!"

"Well, yes, my father is wealthy. He owns a very big cotton farm – kind of a plantation, though no one in the county really calls it that anymore. Plus, my grandfather had made a lot of money, which Daddy inherited. I will just tell you this, Alice…money doesn't mean much when everyone in the family is miserable. I think I was the only person in the family who *wasn't* miserable till I got shipped here. Now I'm miserable, too."

"Oh, Rose. Don't be miserable. Look around you. All these girls are in the same situation. They might not be overly joyful about it, but everyone takes it in stride. It's just another thing in life we have to get through. Most of us were caught making foolish decisions and got into this situation. Not everybody…." Alice stopped talking.

"What do you mean?" Rose asked.

"A couple of the girls here were raped. One girl who is nearly due was raped, and another girl who just got here a couple of weeks ago was raped," Alice replied, lowering her voice. "I'm not supposed to know that, of course, so you can never say anything about it, ok?"

"Oh, how horrible - pregnant by a rapist!" Rose said.

Alice snorted. "Huh! If I was pregnant by some jerk who raped me, I wouldn't be pregnant for very long, I can assure you that."

Rose was uncomfortable with the turn the discussion had taken. The idea of being raped was too terrible to think about.

"Oh, this is a horrid, depressing conversation. Alice, let's think about something fun. What could we do that would be fun for all the girls? Could we have some kind of party or…I don't know. Would Mrs. Kellogg allow us to plan anything like that? She's always such a stick in the mud."

Alice was interested in the idea.

"She might. She's definitely not one to think of something 'fun' herself, but Miss Sullivan might be, and we could run it through her. What kind of party were you thinking about?"

Rose rubbed her belly and said, "What about a Fourth of July barbeque? How could anyone object to something like that? Even Mrs. Kellogg would approve something patriotic, I bet."

"Great idea," Alice replied. "We could have hotdogs and hamburgers and baked beans and potato salad and watermelon…all stuff they'd never feed us any other time, that's for sure!"

Both girls laughed, stood up, and headed for the house. "Let's talk to Miss Sullivan tomorrow morning about the idea," Rose said. "Maybe we'll be able to cheer up some of these girls."

Alice stopped walking. "Rose, for a girl who's had a lot to be sad about, you feel like trying to cheer up the others?" She smiled broadly. "Now that's what I call a demonstration of love."

"Nah," Rose brushed it off with a wave of her hand. "I don't know about all that…I'm a Southern girl and I just need some barbeque."

12

Winchester was not a bad location for the summer months, especially if you were pregnant. It wasn't quite as humid as North Carolina, though it could get awfully hot. The girls in the home who had come from up north felt the difference and complained bitterly about the intemperate climate they were forced to endure. Rose took it all in good-naturedly; she had been in a *truly* intemperate climate in her lifetime. Only one state away from home, Virginia weather felt like a vacation to her.

She was starting to 'pop out' now. That's what the girls called it. Her abdomen protruded in front of her and pulled her back so that almost every morning, she woke up with a back ache. The nurses advised her to make sure she did some back stretching when she got up, after she had gotten fully awake, and to make sure she did plenty of walking.

"Walking really helps," Deb told her. "Make sure you're standing up good and straight when you go for a walk. What kind of chores are you being assigned now, by the way?"

"Yesterday I mopped floors," Rose answered.

"Well, that will need to come to an end before too much longer. Just be careful when you're doing any chores like that. It's ok - don't be worried about it – women regularly do this kind of thing when they're pregnant, but you just want to be careful about how vigorous you are in completing these tasks. Don't hurry through them or put yourself at risk for falling and things like that," Deb told her. "You're young and strong, but don't overestimate what you're able to do. I'll ask Mrs. Kellogg to think about lessening the load over the next couple of months. We make those recommendations to her as girls are getting farther along in their pregnancies. She usually listens to us on things like this."

About the middle of July, Rose was helping tidy up the big veranda at the back of the home. There were numerous wicker chairs with big pillow seats that needed to be flipped and fluffed, tables with a variety of magazines for the girls to read in their leisure time that needed to be straightened. It happened to be very hot that day – nearly 90 degrees – and within a short time, Rose was feeling tired, over-heated, and nauseated. She had been assigned with Deeny to complete the work, but the young girl was not particularly helpful, mostly sitting down to leaf through the newer magazines while Rose worked.

"Deeny, can you please help me instead of loafing?" Rose asked pointedly. "We're to work together on this, and if we do that, we'll be done quicker. Please...you work on one end of the porch and I'll work on the other. We can meet in the middle."

"This is ridiculous. We're not slaves," Deeny began. "They treat us like we're servants around here or something."

Rose stopped and looked at her. "Listen, they have to keep us busy somehow, and doing some light work is probably good for us. It doesn't do any good to complain. Now let's just get this done and go on about our day."

"Go right ahead, Miss Goody Two Shoes. While you're at it, why don't you weed the garden and bale some hay?" It was obvious that Deeny would be no help on this hot day, getting hotter by the minute, it seemed.

Rose went back to her work. She knew that *someone* had to accomplish this or they would both be blamed for not getting it done. Mrs. Kellogg would not mince words, and she might even restrict privileges. It wasn't worth the grief, so Rose worked away, sweeping the porch as the final task. She thought about Miss Stella and the other people who worked for the Caswell family. Did they feel like slaves? Had she and her family treated them all well enough? It was during these thoughts that she felt a tensing of the muscles in her lower abdomen. It wasn't painful, but her belly felt very hard. She sat down and put her hand where she had felt the muscles tightening up, but the feeling was gone.

She started to stand back up when the muscles tightened again. She recognized that she was having contractions. The nurses had taught her about what contractions might feel like, but this was too soon, she thought. Too soon.

"Deeny," Rose called out. "Deeny will you please put down that magazine? I need your help," Rose implored.

"Whatever it is, I'm sure you'll be able to do it just fine without me," Deeny replied, never looking up.

"I'm having contractions! Go get a nurse!" Rose's loud command got Deeny's attention and the young girl looked at her with her mouth hanging open.

"Are you having your baby?" Deeny asked.

"Oh, God, I hope not. Just go get a nurse. Please..." Rose answered.

Deeny disappeared through the back door to the home. It seemed like a long time before she came back with Angie Sweeney. Angie had a little bag of medical supplies with her. With girls in their first pregnancy, she knew that you could never be certain about what you would encounter.

"What's happening, Rose?" Angie asked. "Deeny said you're having contractions?"

"Yes. It just started while I was out here cleaning," Rose began. "I was just finishing sweeping the floor when the first one came on. I sat down for a minute, then another one hit. My belly felt really tight."

"Have you noticed anything like this before?" Angie asked, wrapping a blood pressure cuff around Rose's arm.

"No, this is the first time I felt anything like this." Rose wiped some sweat from her brow.

"Your blood pressure is fine, Rose. How long have you been out here working?" Angie continued her inquiry. "And what kind of jobs have you been doing in this heat?"

"Deeny and I were assigned to clean the veranda this morning. We didn't get out here till after our usual morning activities, so now I suppose it's what – almost noon? No wonder I'm so hot."

Angie looked at Deeny. The younger girl didn't have a bead of sweat on her. Angie turned back to Rose.

"Who's been doing all the work out here? Did you clean the whole porch by yourself? Rose, wicker furniture isn't as heavy as inside furniture, but it still has some weight to it, and in this heat...time for you to quit for today." She turned to face Deeny. "It doesn't appear to me that you've done quite your share out here, Deeny, but I can tell you this...Rose is done for today. You'll have to finish whatever she didn't get done. She's going in to lie down. Understand?"

Deeny shook her head affirmatively, but as soon as Angie turned back, Rose saw Deeny stick out her tongue like a petulant child. A baby having a baby, she thought.

"Rose, I'm pretty sure you're just having Braxton-Hicks contractions. It's nothing to worry about. Let's get you in the house and up to your room; then I'll explain a little more about it, ok?" Angie helped her stand up. "Are you having any contractions now?"

"No, I haven't had one since I asked Deeny to go get you."

"Ok, that kind of confirms my thinking even more. Come on. Let's go in," Angie said, and they left Deeny pouting on the porch.

Once they were in her room, Rose asked, "Angie, do you know how old Deeny is? She acts like a bratty little child."

"I'm not supposed to share that kind of information, Rose, but I'm telling you anyway. She *is* a child. She's only fourteen."

"Oh, my God!" Rose sat down on the edge of her bed. "No wonder she acts the way she does. And she's going to have a baby?"

"Well, yeah, she sure is." Angie chuckled. "If you guys aren't here having babies, I don't have a job."

"You know what I mean. She's so young," Rose said.

"Yes, she is. She's *too* young. She's one of the girls who really *needs* to let someone have her baby, in my opinion. She's in no way capable of caring for a baby from an emotional standpoint. She's just a kid herself. That one's not had an easy life," Angie told her.

Rose wondered if Deeny was one of the girls who had been raped, but was afraid to ask and knew that Angie wouldn't divulge that kind of information anyway.

"Tell me some more about these contractions," Rose said, changing the subject.

"Braxton-Hicks contractions, they're called. They're harmless, Rose. A lot of people say they're 'practice contractions' – your uterus getting ready for what's to come. They happen a little more in the last trimester, but I have known a lot of girls who had them in their second trimester, too, so you're not abnormal in any way. Here's the important thing I want you to know…they happen more when you've been really active or working very hard – that kind of thing. If you are having them, just rest for a little bit. If you have work to do, just take regular breaks. Here's another very important thing to remember. Braxton-Hicks contractions are not regular. I mean, they don't have a rhythm to them. They come and go intermittently.

When you go into labor, the contractions will come on a regular cycle. Rest won't make them go away. If you have contractions like that, you need to let us know right away. It's too soon for you to go into real labor."

"I know. That's why this kind of scared me today. I don't want anything bad to happen to my baby," Rose said.

Angie turned her back to Rose for a minute, then turned again to face her. "Please listen carefully to what I'm about to say to you. You know I would never say anything to hurt you or to try to convince you to do something that's against your will, right?"

Rose nodded. Angie and Deb had been some of the kindest people she ever met.

Angie spoke quietly. "Rose, homes like Weingarten exist for one purpose and one purpose only. To take babies from girls who don't want them or shouldn't have them and place them into the arms of parents who really do want them and can't have them on their own. When I hear you talk about 'your' baby, I worry that you have not come to this understanding, or that if you have, you haven't accepted it."

"I know why I'm here," Rose said, her voice sad. "No, I don't suppose I have accepted it fully. In my heart of hearts, I want to keep my baby and marry Rafe. The longer I'm here, though, without seeing him or anyone in my family, the more it feels like I'm just on my own, trying to figure it out. It makes me more depressed than I can tell you. I try to hide it from Dr. Pickens or else he'd have me on some kind of medicine, and I don't want to take anything but my vitamins. So…I just try to remember this little baby all the time, think about things that are beautiful, stay outside as much as I can in the fresh air – that kind of thing. I've thought about trying to run away from here, but where would I go?"

"You're in a tough spot, that's for sure. Just remember this: in the end, no one can really force you to give up your baby, Rose – not even Mrs. Kellogg or her cronies. You don't have to sign those adoption papers," Angie said.

"What happens if you don't sign the papers?" Rose asked.

"I don't know," Angie said, shaking her head as she started to leave. "In all the years I've worked here, I've never seen it happen. The option is never chosen. Don't forget what I told you about the contractions, ok?" She smiled. "Rose, you could be the first to choose the option, but you didn't hear that from me," she said. Then she closed the door behind her, leaving Rose to reconsider what she had assumed was a foregone conclusion.

13

On a hot, sunny Monday morning in late August, Mrs. Kellogg came into Rose's room and stood just inside the door.

"Rose, we are completely out of space here at the home, and I have to bring you a roommate today." There was no asking permission, only a pronouncement from the home's administrator.

"I thought my father had paid for a private accommodation," Rose said. "I'm not really up to having anyone in such close quarters."

"I can't help it," Mrs. Kellogg replied. "I have no choice. You're not the only young woman in the world who has gotten into trouble. Apparently there are so many of you that there's 'no room at the inn,' as one might say. There's no room at *any* inns. That tells you something about the moral state of our country, I suppose. The fact remains, we'll be admitting another young lady to share these accommodations. You will need to consolidate your belongings to one side of the room. You may choose which side that will be since you were the first occupant. See to it that this is accomplished before afternoon, please. I'll deal with the financial issue with your father." With that, Mrs. Kellogg turned heel and closed the door behind her.

Rose looked around the room. It wasn't the type of living quarters she had enjoyed back home, but she had made it as comfortable as she possibly could. Father had made sure she had some of her belongings…her jewelry box, a stuffed teddy bear she had received as a gift when she was little. On one of the girls' shopping outings, she had purchased new curtains for the room – white with little embroidered daisies. They made her think of her mother. She had a small bookshelf with some of her favorite books: Gone With the Wind, Jane Eyre, Wuthering Heights, and The House at Pooh Corner. That one was for the baby. She had a nice comfortable sitting chair, as well. Once Rose had known there was no choice for her but to stay at Cordelia Weingarten, she had just tried to make the best of things. She still had hope then.

There were two windows in the room. Clearly, the kindest thing to do would be to divide the room so that each person had a window to look out. She wasn't sure she should be moving her bed all by herself. She decided if she alternated scooting the head and foot of the bed across the wood floor, she might be able to accomplish the task without causing any problems. She proceeded carefully, not wanting to incur the wrath of Mrs. Kellogg because of scratches on the floor. Once that was done, she moved her sitting chair in front of the window closest to her bed. She loved sitting and just looking out the window or reading, feeling the warmth of the sun on her face and arms.

Rose arranged and rearranged a few things so that they were still neat and organized, but compacted into her own space. She wondered about her new roommate. Would she bring very much with her? She knew she was going to have to make accommodations for this person, and she wanted her to feel welcome. It was hard enough to go through a pregnancy all by yourself. Maybe she could make a friendship out of this situation. She had always had a lot of girlfriends at school…it was one of the things she missed most about being stuck at the Weingarten home. She had not really gotten close to anyone.

Before long, two maintenance workers brought another twin bed to the room. It had plain white sheets and a lumpy-looking pillow. Rose knew that pillow would be worthless to sleep on. She walked over and ran her hands over the sheets. They were made of the cheapest cotton…North Carolina mills would never let such a rough, uncomfortable product leave the plant. She already felt sorry for the girl who was walking into this situation.

After lunch, Rose went to exercise class and then returned to her room to read. She had no chores to do, and she was glad for a lazy afternoon. She was reading and had almost drifted off to sleep when the door opened. Mrs. Kellogg entered with a pregnant girl in tow.

"Rose C., meet Elizabeth E. I trust you'll welcome her warmly and help her get settled in. I'll see both of you at dinner." Mrs. Kellogg left the two of them standing there, just looking at each other.

"Well, the first thing I'll tell you is that no one calls me Elizabeth. I go by Liz, and I'd appreciate it if you just use that name. If you call me Elizabeth, I won't even answer. No one calls me that." She was breezy, nonchalant. She had beautiful green eyes, outlined by heavy black eyeliner and dark, short, spiky hair. Rose had never seen a haircut like that in her entire life. She wore jeans and a blouse, but the blouse was tight around her belly. Rose wondered if she had any maternity clothes. Her shoes were white sneakers with no shoe strings in them.

"I'm Rose and I only go by Rose. Welcome. I guess you can see the room's not overly large, but I'm sure we'll be able to make out just fine." Rose smiled at her new roommate.

"I heard there's a whole list of rules we have to go by," Liz said. "I'm not much of a rule-follower or I guess I wouldn't be here." She laughed loudly and flopped down on her bed. "I'm assuming this one is mine since it only has sheets on it," she said. "How'd you get such a nice bedspread?"

"Well, actually, my father sent it for me. I bought the curtains, though. Hope you don't mind daisies," Rose said.

"I don't care one way or the other, to tell you the truth. When's dinner? I'm starving," Liz commented. "I'm hungry all the time now!"

"Dinner isn't till six. I have some snacks in a drawer if you would like something to tide you over," Rose offered.

"Hot damn! That would be great!" Liz blurted. Rose opened the desk drawer to show Liz what she had available.

"Cookies. I'll have a couple of cookies." Liz grabbed a package of Oreos and opened it. "Thank you so much! I must be growing a monster child in here." She clapped her hand on her protruding abdomen. "Come on little drummer boy, dance for your mama!"

Rose stared, dumbfounded. She had never met anyone quite like Liz E. before, that's for sure. "How do you know you're having a boy?"

"Oh, I don't," Liz replied. "I just have this feeling that it's a boy, and his daddy was a drummer for a band called The Wizards. They're weren't famous or anything, but I thought they would be in time."

"What happened to them?" Rose asked.

"The lead guitar player died of a heroin overdose and the rest of the band just split. They couldn't hang without him, I guess. My boyfriend's name was Jimmy, but he wasn't much of a boyfriend, really. He was just a guy I hung out with and slept with, obviously."

She smiled a toothy grin, displaying a gap between her two front teeth. "I kind of miss him in some ways. He doesn't even know we're having a kid and I'm due in just a month or so. At least I think."

"You mean he left you altogether?" Rose was incredulous.

"Oh yeah, man. He's gone. One of the other guys said he went to Seattle." Liz picked up her suitcase. "I have his picture in here. I'll show it to you."

Liz opened her beat-up suitcase. There were hardly any clothes in it. She had a pair of sandals, a few tie-dyed shirts, and a couple of long skirts. That was it. Liz pulled out a picture, wrinkled and frayed along the edges. "Here he is. Jimmy. This picture is kind of messed up." She handed it to Rose.

A young man with long hair stared out from the picture at Rose. He did not smile. His eyes were soft, but his jaw was square and hard. He was not unattractive, but kind of dangerous-looking.

"Nice picture," was all Rose could muster.

"Yeah, he is quite a guy," Liz said. "Too bad we couldn't stay together."

"Do you think he might come back?" Rose asked, surprised at how open this conversation was. After all, they were still really strangers.

"Nah, he'll never be back. That's why I'm here. He left about $200 in the apartment when he took off. It was mostly change, but that was still good because otherwise, I'd have been out selling weed or something. I got a job at a record shop and saved every penny I could, but I don't have any way to get medical care or anything like that, so I put all the money I saved into this place. I didn't think they were going to take me at first. Our friend Mrs. Kellogg said they didn't have any room, but then she decided they did after all, so here I am."

"Well, Liz, I hope you'll forgive me for being so blunt, but Mrs. Kellogg is a tough one, and I'm going to give you a couple of pieces of advice. Is that ok?' Rose wanted to help this young woman stay out of any more trouble than she was already in.

"Sure. I can take it," Liz answered.

"First of all, you've got to read this rule paper we have around here. You've got to live by these rules or you'll be sorry you didn't. I am not kidding about this. We have a pretty strict schedule we have to follow, so you'll have to get used to that, too. Everything about our stay here is guarded, it seems like. It feels like prison in many ways, or a nunnery. I shouldn't say that. I don't know a thing about nuns. Anyway, you'll get used to feeling like you're in prison. It becomes your only option. Or at least they make you feel it is."

Liz just stared at her. Rose took a breath and continued. "Be ready for a brainwashing job. You get the brainwashing treatment right from your very first day. The only way I got through it was to remember how much my boyfriend and I love each other and to remember that someday, he and I will be back together. You have to create your own hope around this place."

"Well," Liz said, "that's a pretty gloomy perspective. Listen, I can deal with the toughest of them, so little Mrs. Kellogg doesn't scare me. And as far as rules, I've never followed any except those I made for myself or otherwise agreed to. I'm sure I'll be fine, but I appreciate your advice, I really do. I'll do my best to not make trouble. I've got to get this little drummer boy delivered and get on with life."

Rose was amazed at the cavalier approach to childbirth Liz seemed to take, but she was also mildly amused. "I think we're going to get along just fine, Liz E.," she said. "Dinner is at 6 sharp. You better get ready."

"I'm ready right now! It's only 5, though. Yikes! Can I have a couple more Oreos?" Liz asked with her hand held out.

Rose laughed. "Sure, but just another thing…they watch our calories like hawks around here. Gain too much weight and you're going to be subjected to the nutrition lecture which is about as interesting as watching paint dry."

Liz smiled her gap-toothed grin. "I'll just make sure I take a crap before I get weighed."

Rose laughed harder than she had any time since she had been at the home. "Oh, Lord! I have never met anyone like you, Liz E. Hey, I think I'll just call you Lizzy. Liz E. Lizzy. What do you think? Oh, except in front of Mrs. Kellogg. I'm sure she'll demand that you be called Elizabeth."

"Lizzy. I like it. 'Lizzy E. took an axe'…" Liz chuckled.

"Don't you even dare to finish!" Rose cried, laughing.

Liz went into the bathroom to shower. Rose sat down and considered this strange, funny girl she had just met. She was kind of wild and rebellious – Rose admired people who didn't give a darn about what other people thought and wished she had that trait.

Liz walked out to her side of the room, brushing her hair, completely naked. Rose was shocked and turned away, pretending to straighten up her bed linens.

"Hey, don't feel too shy," Liz said, noticing Rose's embarrassment. "I like being au naturel whenever I can. It's just our bodies."

Rose glanced her way and said, "I'm a little on the shy side, myself." She noticed a tattoo of a rose on Liz's back, near her left shoulder. "You have a tattoo! A tattoo of a rose!"

"Yeah, kind of a prophecy, huh? I got it once when I was drunk. It hurt like hell, but you know…the stuff you do when you're drunk…." Liz started getting dressed in one of her tie dyes.

"I've never been drunk, though I have had drinks," Rose said. "Sometimes I wish I *could* get drunk."

"Aw, it's not worth the pain the next day. Trust me on that." Liz was ready to go. "Take me to the food!"

Rose smiled at Liz, but she was thinking about what Mrs. Kellogg might say about Liz' clothes. Good thing she wouldn't be able to see that tattoo.

They arrived in the dining room with a few minutes to spare. Rose found a couple of chairs near the end of the table farthest away from Mrs. Kellogg, hoping to spare Liz any criticism over dinner. The girls sat down by one another. Rose noticed Deeny giving Liz dirty looks, already disdainful of this new girl without even knowing her.

"Lizzy, during dinner, there is NO conversation," Rose began. "We are served our dinner by a wait staff, but they bring in covered plates and no one takes the lid off their plate till every single girl is served. Then we eat. When you're done, you can cover your plate back up, but then you have to just sit here till everyone is done. It's just how it goes."

"Good God, it does sound like a prison or something!" Lizzy said. "Are you serious?"

"Serious as a stroke," Rose answered. "Listen, I'll tell you what a really nice girl named Alice told me when I first got here: you'll be ok. It's scary at first and you don't know what in the world to expect, so you just take it a day at a time. It will be ok."

"It better be. I paid a pretty penny to get in here. I have nothing left, so this has got to work out," Liz said.

Girls were filing in, so Rose and Liz turned themselves to the table and sat quietly, waiting for the room to finish filling and for Mrs.

Kellogg to show up. There was quiet chatter among the other girls, but Liz remained silent and observant. Rose reached over and squeezed her arm.

Mrs. Kellogg entered the room, stood at the head of the table, and as usual, conducted grace. Rose glanced at Liz, who did not bow her head, but continued looking at the other residents. When the final "amen" came, Liz looked over at Rose, and for the first time, Rose saw that Liz might not be as confident as she first appeared to be. She smiled at Liz, nodding an affirmation to let Liz know everything would be ok.

The food began appearing, and Liz forgot that she was supposed to wait for everyone to receive their plates. Deeny snorted, amused, as Liz immediately took the lid off her plate and began eating. The clinking of her fork on her plate drew the attention of Mrs. Kellogg, who looked at Liz with surprise, then disgust. Rose waited for the admonition from the head of the table, but none came. By that time, everyone had been served. They ate in silence. Liz fairly gobbled her food down, as if she were starving. When she was done, she remembered to sit quietly till everyone had finished.

Upon dismissal, Rose tried to steer Liz past Mrs. Kellogg, but she wasn't quick enough. Mrs. Kellogg reached out and grabbed Lizzy's arm as she walked past, even though Rose was between them.

"Elizabeth, I'd like you to stay behind for a moment." Her voice was firm.

"Ok, no problem," Liz replied, but she looked anxious.

"I'll wait right outside," Rose said as she walked on.

After all the girls had exited the dining room, Mrs. Kellogg closed the door. Rose could hear muffled voices through the door, nothing too loud, so maybe it was all right. Several minutes passed.

The door swung open and Mrs. Kellogg bustled past her. She looked into the dining room for Liz and found her sitting in Mrs. Kellogg's chair, looking stunned.

"Are you all right?" Rose asked.

"Let's go to our room and I'll tell you about it," Liz said very quietly.

They walked up the steps quickly. It was clear Liz didn't want to stay on the first floor any longer than she had to.

"What a witch!" Liz exploded, once they had arrived in their room. "How can someone so mean be the head of an unwed mothers home, for Pete sake? She got on me about starting to eat too soon. She got on me about my makeup and hair. She got on me about my clothes. What am I going to do? I don't have any clothes besides these and I sure don't have any money for new ones. Heck, half the things I have don't fit, so I'm stuck with just these few things that *do* fit. Holy crap. What am I going to do?"

Rose thought for a minute. "Well, the eating thing was a slip, but you'll remember that next time. As for hair and makeup, just tone it all down a little bit. Wear less eyeliner and just kind of smooth your hair down a little. Always keep that tattoo covered up, that's for sure. When it comes to the clothes, that might be an area where I can help you."

"What do you mean? Do you have some extras?" Liz asked.

"Not really. I'm trying not to buy a lot of maternity stuff, to tell you the truth. But...I have an allowance each month from my father. We can buy you a few things when we get to go on our next shopping trip. I think it's this Thursday, as a matter of fact." Rose consulted her calendar. "Oh, no...it's not till September. You can just borrow some stuff from me if you need to till then. Well anyway, those of us who want to go downtown take a small bus and all shop together. Since we're not allowed to go unescorted, we all have to go to every shop every other girl wants to go to, but it's kind of fun and gets us out of this place for a little while."

"I don't know about taking your money...that seems not cool to me." Liz looked away. Rose thought she might be embarrassed about not having money.

"Believe me, it would make me really happy to help you pick out some clothes. That would be fun for me, honest." Rose sat down on the edge of her bed. "It will remind me of going shopping with my girlfriends back in Kinston. Please let me do this for you. I never use all the money Daddy sends me every month - honest."

"I have to think about it a little, but...well, I don't really feel like getting the riot act read to me again. Maybe if we could just get a couple of things...." Liz trailed off.

Rose jumped up and went over to give Liz a hug. "Oh, Lizzy, it will be the most fun I've had since I got here, I'm sure of it. Now listen, you better start reading your rule paper. Tomorrow morning comes fast and you'll have a full day ahead of you, trust me. Tomorrow the brainwashing begins, *hard*. The only genuinely kind people who work here are the nurses up in the medical ward. You'll like them. My favorites are Nurse White, who will insist that you call her Deb, and Nurse Sweeney, who goes by Angie."

"Rose, I think I'm pretty lucky to have you around right now. Thank you for trying to help me," Liz said quietly, eyes down. "My parents kicked me out years ago, and I've got no one." Her eyes welled up. "Jimmy ditched me, too, and I have a feeling he wouldn't have stayed even if he knew I was knocked up. I really have no one. Listen, what do you mean by brainwashing?"

"I mean that everyone you talk to except the nurses will make you feel like you're some kind of wild child who can't control her desires. They will tell you that you're abnormal and make you have psychological counseling which is mostly the psychologist telling you what a deviant you are. The social worker will start pushing you to give up your baby for adoption, and believe me, they never back down on this stuff. You hear it every time you go for an appointment. I've gotten to the place where I just nod my head, say as little as possible, and let them do the talking. Every once in a while they ask you a question, so you *have* to listen just to be able to answer, but other than that, I don't tell them much."

"Don't you want to put your baby up for adoption?" Liz asked.

Rose hesitated for a minute. "Not really, but I'm at a place that I don't know what else I could do. I'm afraid to try to run away from here. I don't have any money except what Daddy sends, and how long would that last, paying for an apartment and food and a car? I don't have a job and probably couldn't get one since I'm considered 'damaged goods.' And how would I have this baby? I wouldn't have a doctor or a safe place to have the baby. If only my boyfriend knew where I was. I know he'd come get me and we'd be all right."

"What's your boyfriend's name?" Liz asked.

"Rafe. Rafe Whitfield. He's the most wonderful man in my life," Rose answered. "He's kind and smart and funny. You'd love him."

"I'm sure he's great. He doesn't know where you are, huh?"

"No," Rose replied. "I believe my father has made certain that *no one* knows where I am, not even my mother or brother."

"Wow! He must have been pretty mad about you getting pregnant," Liz said.

"Mad doesn't begin to describe it. My father is a very difficult man. *Very* difficult. Still, I love and understand him somehow. I hate that I hurt him this way, but I wish he was more understanding." Rose thought for a minute. "I keep hoping that he'll come around, come get me and take me home, but I'm almost due now and he still hasn't showed up. Just keeps sending me an allowance. Isn't that great?"

"It's better than being broke and not knowing where your next meal is coming from," Liz said.

"True," Rose said. "I'm luckier than a lot of girls."

"Hell, yeah. You're looking at one of them," Liz smiled. "Ok, I gotta get reading Mrs. Kellogg's rule list. I can see I don't want to cross that woman."

"Lizzy, I'm glad you're my roommate. I really am," Rose said. "We're going to be good friends, I can see that right now."

"Thank you Rose. That's one thing I've not had a lot of in this world…friends." Liz picked up the rule paper and went to lie down on her bed to read.

Rose sat down in her own chair and picked up her copy of Wuthering Heights. She hadn't read it in a while. The story felt similar to her own in many respects, and it had been painful to read the story when she first arrived at Weingarten. Now things would get a little better. She had a new friend.

14

It had been four months, and Rafe didn't know his way around Chicago in September any better than when he first arrived in June. He was constantly lost and asking for directions. Thankfully, people here would kindly provide them. Midwesterners had turned out to be as friendly as southerners.

He had been lucky enough to get hired at the Chicago Tribune. He spent his twentieth birthday working in the mailroom. He wasn't writing any articles, but it was a start, and he was learning a lot about journalism and the newspaper business along the way. He was making enough money to get an apartment and meet his needs for living. He enrolled in a class at Northwestern - may as well start his college education. He didn't need much in the way of entertainment because all of his spare time was spent trying to locate Rose, who was supposedly staying with Ham Caswell's sister...Rose's Aunt Marnie. He had learned who Aunt Marnie was. She held some degree of socialite status in Chicago and her name was in the Tribune related to various social events. However, her location was almost impossible to discover. Rafe once talked about it to one of the reporters; his advice had painted a bleak picture for Rafe.

"Buddy, if you can find someone who can give you an address, you're a better man than I. These rich people don't want anyone to know where they live. They don't want people showing up at their doorsteps asking for a handout, not that I blame them. They like to go to their fancy fundraisers and get their name in the paper, then go into hiding. Most of them have skeletons they don't want to let out of the closet, so except for the big social soirée, staying out of the limelight is the smartest thing they can do," the reporter had told him.

Rafe didn't give up that easy. He watched the paper for past events and read the article associated with that event, looking for even the smallest clue. He watched for upcoming social events which Aunt Marnie might attend. He made it a point to meet the social editor, Melissa McCoy. She was friendly, and she was kind of cute, too. Rafe thought if he wasn't in up to his heart with Rose, he might find her more interesting. He met her for a drink after work one day at The Billy Goat Tavern, right down the street from the Trib. She was a few minutes late, but he was waiting at the bar.

"What kept you?" Rafe asked. "Meeting with the managing editor?"

"No, I got a last-minute call about a wingding coming up. It's a formal affair to raise money for a new children's charity – Special Olympics. It's for disabled kids…gives them a chance to compete against other disabled kids in different sports. It's a new organization, really," Melissa told him. "I guess there will be professional athletes involved, which gives it even more pizzazz, and frankly, more credibility with those who have money to donate."

"It sounds like a good charity. Who all is involved from sports?" Rafe asked.

"I'm not really sure yet, but Dick Butkus was mentioned. I think they're just getting it going. That's why they need to raise money," Melissa answered. "You know they had the first Special Olympics at Soldier Field in July, but that was a lot of Eunice Kennedy Shriver's doing. Now they're trying to get a formal group here in Chicago."

"Well, it sounds like a really good thing, so I hope they accomplish it." Rafe turned to the bartender. "Can we get a couple of beers?"

Once the bartender produced beers from the tap, cold and frothy, Rafe tried to make an approach to the subject he really wanted to talk about. "What's it like to go to those fancy balls?" he asked. "I'd never make it with that crowd."

"It's nothing to do with me, I can tell you that. My mom and dad were well-off, so we attended a lot of those events when I was a kid. You get to know people. A lot of John Q. Publics make it sound like it's just a bunch of snobs getting together, but they're not a bad lot…no different from the rest of us, really. They just happen to have money. Some of them are stingy with it, but a lot of them are really generous."

"How about Marnie Caswell Duke? Have you ever met her?" Rafe asked.

"Why, yes, I have. She's one of the nice ones. She gives a lot of money away to a whole bunch of charities in this town. How do you know her?" Melissa quizzed.

"I don't really, but I'd sure like to meet her. Her brother lived in my town – in fact, he owns half the town, now that I think about it. He's not so great, but I've always heard nice things about her." Rafe hoped his face and voice wouldn't give him away. This was as close as he'd ever gotten to any information about the elusive Aunt Marnie.

"You should come with me sometime. You could be my escort. Of course, you'd probably have to do some stuff like take pictures, collect the correct spelling of peoples' names and all that. I'll tell you what. Why don't you plan on doing the Special Olympics thing with me? I'm sure Mrs. Duke would support that kind of thing. Maybe you could meet Butkus, too. You know my photographer, John? He'd probably love the night off. It's not exactly his scene, but he has to go where I go." Melissa laughed. "He'll be happy as a clam if I tell him he doesn't have to put on a tux."

"You've got a deal," Rafe said. "Can you introduce me if Marnie's there?"

Melissa smiled. "Sure, and I'll bet you dollars-to-doughnuts she'll be there. Like I said, she's one of the good ones. She gives a lot of money away."

They finished their beers and said good night. Rafe was jubilant. After all this time, he would finally get to meet Marnie Caswell Duke and find his Rose.

And so it was that on September 21, 1968, Rafe showered and shaved, spit-polished his good black shoes, put on his rented tux, and hailed a cab. He hardly ever took a taxi, but tonight he did not want to have to find his way around Chicago. He was skittish as a cat; so much so that he momentarily thought about backing out, but he knew he had to push his anxiety aside; this was his only path to Rose.

He went straight to the Palmer House, where he was to meet Melissa. When he arrived, she was not there. He paced nervously on the sidewalk in front of the famed venue. After a few minutes, she arrived by cab.

"Hey, come get this camera, Rafe," she called. He did as he was told. Melissa looked pretty, and he told her so.

"You look pretty darn good yourself," Melissa answered. "I mean it. You clean up well." She smiled. "Are you ready for this? It can be a little intimidating first time out."

79

"I'm as ready as I'll ever be," Rafe said. "Thankfully, I've had a little practice with the camera recently."

"Hey, so I heard. They're letting you out of the mailroom now, huh? That's great. I hope they increased your pay," Melissa kidded.

"Well, as a matter of fact, I did get a little raise – not much, but every penny helps. I'm actually getting to help write a small story here and there," Rafe told her. "I still really need to go to journalism school. I'm taking a couple of classes but I just don't have a lot of dough, so it's slow-going."

"Maybe you'll meet a benefactor here. Maybe Marnie Caswell Duke will try to help a local boy get educated," Melissa smiled. "You just never know about some of these people…."

They walked into the Grand Ballroom and Rafe caught his breath. He truly had never seen such a beautiful ballroom or so many beautiful people. He had to stand still one minute and take it in.

"Amazing, isn't it? Believe me, by the end of the evening, everyone will know your name and will try to make sure you know theirs…they will be looking for it in the paper in a day or two." Melissa took his arm. "Let's go meet some people and take some pictures."

Melissa coasted through the crowd, it seemed. She was completely at home among these impeccably dressed people, conversing as casually as if they were family. She introduced Rafe to everyone she talked to. They posed for pictures, and Rafe snapped away. He double checked the spelling of names, as he had been instructed to do. He was having fun, even though it was definitely work. He met a lot of people, and to his own surprise, they seemed as nice as Melissa had described.

After a couple of hours had passed, Rafe noticed a lady he had not seen earlier. She was just receiving a glass of champagne from one of the waiters when he heard another lady approach her and call her Marnie. His heart skipped just a beat, and he took a deep breath. Melissa was talking to another patron, and he hated to interrupt her, so he waited as patiently as he could. He was afraid the object of interest would disappear before he had a chance to talk to her. He felt the seconds ticking by like hours.

Finally, Melissa broke loose from the man who was monopolizing her. "Rafe, you look like you've seen a ghost. Are you ok?"

He replied, "Sure, I'm ok. I just saw a new lady come in. We haven't taken her picture yet. She's right over there near the bar. She has a glass of champagne in her hand and a black dress on."

"Well, you've successfully described just about every woman here. Where is she? Point me in the right direction," Melissa said.

Rafe tried to motion with his head towards Marnie. Melissa looked in that direction, confused, but when she saw Marnie, she stopped and put her hand on Rafe's arm. "That's her. That's Marnie Caswell Duke. Shall I introduce you?"

Rafe could hardly get his breath. "Give me one minute."

"What in the name of all that is holy is wrong with you?" Melissa teased. "You'd think she was the queen of England or something. Come on. She'll get lost in this crowd if we don't make a move."

They walked to where Marnie was standing. She was a tall woman, like her brother, Hamilton Caswell. She was a large-boned woman, too, somewhat imposing. The big difference Rafe noticed was a kindness in her face that he had never seen in Hamilton's face.

"Good evening, Mrs. Duke," Melissa began. "It's so wonderful to see you!"

"My, my, little Melissa McCoy. How's your mama and daddy?" Marnie still had her Southern accent. She seemed delighted to see Melissa.

"Oh, they're as fit as a fiddle. They're ready for grandkids and I don't even have a husband, yet," Melissa replied. "They keep reminding me that I'm getting over the hill as far as having children. You know how they are."

"Oh, yes I most certainly do! But they're so lovely. Are they here tonight?" Marnie asked, looking around.

"No. Father has had a touch of bronchitis and the doctor told him to behave himself for a while, so they're at home. Listen, I'm being rude. This is my photographer, Rafe Whitfield."

"Whitfield? I know that name from back home." Marnie momentarily had a puzzled look on her face, studying Rafe and trying to remember. "You couldn't be Glenn Whitfield's boy, could you?"

"Why yes ma'am, that's exactly right. Glenn Whitfield is my father," Rafe replied.

Melissa excused herself. "I'm going to go get something to drink while you two catch up."

Marnie squealed like a little girl. "My lands, I can't believe it! I used to have a crush on your father. He was friends with my brother, Hamilton. Do you know my brother?"

Rafe stuttered, "Y-y-yes. I do know your brother."

"He's having a few health problems right now. I haven't been home to see him for two years, but we talk on the phone occasionally. Do you know Stuart and Rose? Did you go to the same school?"

Rafe cleared his throat. "Why yes, I do. Rose and I were in the same class in high school, but we've lost contact. Do you know how she is?" This was the moment he had anticipated all these months. His mouth was so dry, he could barely speak.

"No, I don't, as a matter of fact," Marnie answered him. "She's been away from home, traveling the United States, according to her father. I thought for sure she'd go to State in the fall – that was always her dream. North Carolina State - Wolfpack, all the way!" Marnie smiled.

Rafe stared at her. He felt like he had been gut-punched. He was sure Marnie was telling the truth by the absolute ease with which she made her statements. He almost dropped the camera.

"She's traveling? That's a surprise," was all Rafe could utter at that moment.

"It was a surprise to me, too. You'd think if she was traveling, she'd come see her old Aunt Marnie; but then, she's young and free and her daddy has plenty of money to let her see the world. I suppose she'll get around to me one day. Well, if you'll excuse me, I must go talk to Doris Dennison. I enjoyed meeting you and talking about back home a little bit."

Rafe forced a smile. "I enjoyed meeting you, too. I should get your picture before you go. Do you mind posing?"

"Not at all, though the Tribune doesn't need another picture of this old mug." Marnie removed her glasses, straightened her fur stole, and smiled at the camera. Rafe snapped the shot and she said, "Goodbye, then, Rafe Whitfield. When you talk to your father, please give him my warmest regards."

"I'll be sure to do that," Rafe replied.

She moved into the crowd and was soon lost in a sea of the well-heeled. Rafe realized he was sweating like a pig and went to get a glass of water. He didn't see Melissa anywhere, but he was hoping she was about ready to leave. He got his water and retreated to a corner of the room. Cool air was flowing down from a vent in the ceiling and he was glad for it.

He didn't know how much time had passed before Melissa approached him. "Well, did you get to catch up with Marnie? She's a sweetheart."

"Yes, she is," Rafe said, looking down to avoid eye contact. "Yes, we caught up."

"Did she tell you any deep dark secrets you didn't know?"

Rafe's head shot up and he looked at the cool brunette. She was kidding with him, of course. He smiled.

"Uh, she told me she once had a crush on my father, and I had never heard about that. I guess that's the extent of the secrets." Rafe was doing his best to maintain a placid appearance. He didn't know Melissa well enough to tell her anything about Rose, her father, the baby – any of it. "Hey, is it about time that we can leave?" he asked.

"Well, I'm going to stay, I think. I'm having fun. But you can go on if you want – you don't really need to stay anymore. Can you bring the camera to work Monday?" Melissa was starting to move away.

"Yes, I'll be sure to do that. Or do you want me to take it over there tomorrow so the pictures can get developed?" Rafe asked.

"Gees, that would be great, if you have the time, that is," Melissa said.

"Yeah, it's no problem. I don't live far from the paper." Rafe turned to go, then turned back. "Thanks for bringing me, Melissa. I can't really tell you how much it means to me."

Melissa smiled, but knit her brows together. "What a strange thing to say! Rafe are you ok? Are you sure you didn't learn some deep and grisly secret about your town?"

Rafe smiled and tried to come across more cheerfully. "Oh, I'm just tired. Don't worry – there are no murderers running around loose, no ghosts to haunt Kinston."

"Ok then. I'll see you Monday," and she was off.

Rafe walked out to the sidewalk and hailed a cab. No ghosts to haunt Kinston...only a ghost to haunt him, and where was she?

15

For a few weeks after the Special Olympics party, Rafe functioned in a fog. He ate and drank and slept. He kept going to work but he was unfocused, restless. He was given a little more responsibility at the paper, working on small articles and the occasional news story from city hall. He loved the processes of producing a newspaper, and he was glad for the distraction, but he was not really *living* as any normal person would define it.

He talked with his parents regularly on the phone, but long distance was expensive. He kept them up-to-date on what he was doing in Chicago. He told them about meeting Marnie Caswell Duke, and he knew his parents were just as sad about the outcome of that meeting as he had been.

He had a few outings with Melissa. She was strong, vibrant, and intellectually challenging. She was a good distraction, too. Rafe could tell that she was fond of him, but he knew he'd never be any good for her. He was still in love with Rose and determined to somehow find her and help raise their baby. He had told no one in Chicago of his plight till one evening in October, when he and Melissa met at the Goat, as they called it. Melissa was waiting for him at the bar when he arrived.

"Whatever you're having, I'll have," Rafe said.

"Barkeep, how about another Jack and water?" Melissa called out. "Well, how was your day?" she began, turning to face him.

"Busy. I'm working on a story about kids skateboarding in Grant Park and how some of the older park-goers find it an annoyance and so forth. It's not a headliner, but I'm still consistently getting these small pieces to work on. The more I get, the better I am at the craft, so I'm grateful," Rafe told her.

"Grateful, ok, but are you happy? You look like the weight of the world is on you every time I see you, Rafe." Melissa saw him starting to shake his head 'no' as if he didn't want to get into it. "No, now, let's talk about this for a minute because I get the clear sense that something is eating you up. We've been out a half dozen times since September, and you never really seem to enjoy anything. Do you realize you've never once even tried to kiss me or hold my hand? I'm sorry, but that just doesn't happen to little ol' *me*." She fluttered her eyelids, her pretense at vanity making Rafe smile. She was not a vain person at all.

"I guess I know you well enough to tell you a tale, but are you ready to hear it?" Rafe asked.

"Hey, I opened this can of worms. Let's dig through it. I can take it." Melissa looked around. "Let's find a booth instead of sitting up here. I want to be able to hear what it is you've got behind those eyes."

They walked to an open booth and sat down across from each other. Rafe hesitated for a minute, then began to tell his story, right from the happy beginning to the bloody end. Melissa never said a word, never asked a question. She was intent on him, taking a sip of her drink once in a while. She never even averted her gaze, and Rafe talked without stopping till his story was done. When it was, he leaned back against the seat in the booth and said, "There you have it. Remember at the Special Olympics thing after I talked to Marnie Caswell? You asked me then if I had found out any deep, dark secrets. I had found out a secret all right...I had been duped."

"Do you think that Miss Stella lady you talked about would have lied to throw you off the track?" Melissa finally asked.

"Oh, no. She's as good as gold, she really is. I have no doubt that she really believed Rose was coming here. I don't think she could intentionally lie if she had a gun pointed at her head," Rafe answered. "She overheard some conversation – some erroneous information. I don't know which...it doesn't matter because in the end, I'm in the wrong place and there's a girl out there somewhere getting ready to have my baby soon and I'm not there for her."

Melissa sat back, too, and pondered what she had just learned. Rafe did not disturb her concentration.

"Rafe, do you know how many young women would die to have a guy like you? Do you know how many pregnant, unmarried girls wish they had a guy who wanted to marry them? It's incredible that this Caswell guy would keep you two apart. Honestly, I don't know how many pregnant girls every year are just left alone to fend for themselves. It's a heck of a lot easier for the father of a child to walk away than it is for the mother of a child to walk away. And how can they keep you, the father, from having your rightful access to the child? This guy must be a real bastard." Melissa got quiet again for a minute. "You know, *this* is a story. It really is. Father's rights in the case of an unplanned pregnancy. Have you thought about writing about it?"

"Good grief, no. All of my energy has been spent on trying to find Rose and rescue her from whatever cloistered convent he has her in. I couldn't even think about writing about something like this," Rafe said.

"Well, it's probably not a common story to be truthful. I'm a little older than you, you know, and I've seen far too many girls end up in some back-alley abortion clinic or at the adoption agency when the father of their child recused himself from the responsibility. For such a young guy, you're awfully mature about all this." She paused. "I'll tell you what. It's about time you got some truthful answers about what you may be able to do as the child's father. I know a great attorney – he does family law. I dated him a few times, and we're still good friends. His name is Henry Parker. He's with Steinbaugh, Deters and Parker. They're on North Michigan. I can call him for you and get an appointment. I know he'd make time with you as a favor to me. He's a super nice guy, he really is. I know he would be interested in trying to help with a case like this. What do you say?"

This idea came at Rafe fast. "I don't have a million bucks to pay lawyers." Then he stopped. "Do you really think this fellow could help?"

"I don't know," Melissa said, looking uncertain, "but it's better than trying what you've been doing, right? Face it. How much progress have you made?"

"I know she's not here. That's it." Rafe finished his drink. "If you think you can get me a little time with this guy, why not? I owe you."

"Think nothing of it. I can't guarantee it's going to get you anywhere, though. You know that, right?"

Rafe smiled, and now he really felt like smiling. This young woman had been nothing but kind since he had been in Chicago. "I've not had any guarantees since the beginning. I wouldn't expect any now."

"Then it's done. I'll call him tomorrow," Melissa said. "Want to get something to eat? I'm starved."

"If it's all the same to you, I'd rather just pick up something and head for home. I'm worn out now. This thing is draining the life out of me," Rafe said.

"Gotcha. Rafe Whitfield, you just hang on...all hope is not lost." She reached across the table and grabbed his arm. "*All hope is not lost.*"

Right then, Rafe really could have kissed her. "You're a good friend, Melissa."

"And that's all, isn't it?" She smiled. "At least now I understand why."

* * *

Towards the end of October, Melissa came into the small office where the city reporters worked. Rafe was still doing minor reporting for that group. She walked up to his desk and said, "Got a sec?" She was smiling, excited to tell him something.

"Yeah. It's almost lunch – want to go early?" Rafe replied.

"I can't. I am meeting some ladies over at the Palmer for lunch today. It's part of my social reporting gig, so I can't skip out. Can we just go in the break room or something?" Melissa was fidgeting, anxious to tell him something.

Rafe got up from his desk and walked with Melissa to the break room. He poured a cup of coffee while Melissa started talking.

"I got you an appointment! I knew Henry would see you. What's more, I told him a little about your situation and he was mad as hell. He thinks you have some grounds to...I don't know, sue the Caswells or something. He's anxious to meet you. Here's the thing. He's got real limited time, so you must go tomorrow morning at 9 a.m. sharp. Can you get off work in the morning?"

Rafe thought for a minute. "All I can do is ask...I might be able to come in later. Where again is the office?"

Melissa wrote down the address on a napkin, gave him a little hug and said, "I've got to scoot. Rafe, I really do hope you can get some answers. Wouldn't it just be the greatest happy ending?"

Rafe smiled and said, "I hope I can repay you someday for all this. You've been great to me since the first day I met you."

"Your payback can be your book about this. You're a good writer. Someday you really must tell your story so other fathers in your boat know how to maneuver through the mess," Melissa said. "That's what I'd love to see. A book about the mothers and fathers who are torn apart and what happens to them. Do that - help somebody else. If you don't, this kind of thing will screw up the next generation of unwed mothers and fathers." She winked and went on her way.

Rafe's boss gave him permission to come in late the next day. He tried to stay focused throughout the remaining work hours that afternoon, but he was preoccupied. All that night, he had a hard time sleeping. He dozed, then would wake up with a start, sure he had missed his appointment. Then he would think of a question. He began writing them down so that he wouldn't forget anything in the precious time he would have with the attorney.

Henry Parker's office looked like the Taj Mahal. Rafe was seriously underdressed for an appointment with a man who worked in such an office. But Henry Parker wasn't that kind of man, and as soon as Rafe was introduced by his receptionist, Henry jumped up from behind his desk and came around to meet Rafe, hand extended for a shake.

"How do you do, Rafe? I'm very glad to meet you. Any friend of Melissa's is a friend of mine," Henry began. "Please have a seat. Can I get you a cup of coffee? We keep a percolator right outside the door."

"That would be great. I didn't sleep too well last night, and coffee would be helpful right about now," Rafe replied.

Henry hit an intercom button. "Sally, do you mind bringing in some coffee for us? Bring some cream and sugar, too, would you?" He turned to Rafe. "Let's go ahead and get started. As I'm sure you know, I'm sworn to the highest level of confidence, and my staff must follow suit, so even if Sally comes in while we're talking, she will not repeat anything she hears."

"I wasn't really worried about that at all," Rafe said, "but I appreciate your reassurance."

Just about that time, Sally appeared with a tray with coffee, sugar and cream. She set the tray on a table by the window and left, closing the door behind her.

Henry got up first to go over to the coffee tray, and Rafe followed. As Henry was pouring a cup for them both, he began speaking.

"Let me tell you what I know at this point. You and a young lady got pregnant just prior to graduating from high school. You both wanted to get married but her father wanted nothing to do with that idea. She was whisked away in the dead of night and no one knew for sure where she landed. You thought she was here. Why did you think that?"

"I spoke with the family maid. She's a sweetheart and she told me Rose had come here to stay with an aunt – Marnie Caswell Duke."

"Ah, yes, Marnie. I only know her through social contacts, but she's a dear. She's a very generous patron of the arts and I know she supports other charitable causes as well. And you found out from her recently that your Rose is not here after all?" Henry sat down in his chair and pulled out a legal pad and pen and began writing notes.

"Yes. I attended the Special Olympics ball with Melissa – I went as her photographer. She introduced me to Marnie, who recognized my name from back home. Turns out she had a crush on my old man." Rafe stopped and smiled. "That would give him a chuckle, I'm pretty sure."

Henry smiled, too. "High school crushes…well, listen, let me just ask you this. Trying to find your girl or at least the baby is a tough thing to do. Are you sure *you* don't just have a 'high school crush' on her? Are you sure you want to go through with all this? And Rafe, are you 100% sure you're the father? I'm just asking, so don't be offended."

Rafe never hesitated. "Yes, I'm absolutely sure. For one thing, Rose and I were both virgins when we first…well, you know…and what Rose and I have is more than a crush. I've never met anyone I loved more than her, and I do believe she feels the same way about me. We'd have been married months ago, if her father hadn't gotten in the way."

"What was his objection, anyway?" Henry asked.

"I didn't meet his criteria, particularly his financial criteria," Rafe said. "He told me in no uncertain terms he wasn't happy with my choice of profession and that I'd never marry his daughter."

"What happened after Rose disappeared?" Henry continued his questioning.

"My dad, mom and I all went out to the Caswell estate and kind of surprised them at the dinner hour. My dad and Mr. Caswell were friends in high school, though you would never have known it by the way he talked to my dad. He was bullying and threatening to my dad and mom. I didn't mind so much that he was mad at me – after all, I got his daughter pregnant – but the way he talked to my folks was completely uncalled for. He insulted them in every possible way. It was pretty terrible."

"Ok, I'm getting a picture of this guy. So he's got money? Then he can buy about any high-priced lawyer he wants in order to protect his territory, so to speak. He sounds like a guy who wants to be in control of everything and everyone."

"Yes," Rafe replied, "but I'm not trying to push back at him, truthfully. I just want to find Rose. I'm sure he shipped her off to some unwed mothers home, and you know what happens there…the babies get put up for adoption. I want my child. She's part of me and Rose, and I want my baby to be with both of us."

Henry smiled. "How do you know it's a she? You could have a son in there, you know?"

Rafe had never even really considered that. He always assumed Rose would have a little girl, lovely and sweet as she. "Well," he began, "you're right about that. I hadn't thought about a baby boy that much."

Henry sat quietly for a minute. "Rafe, I have to be honest. I don't know if I can help you; you see, there are a lot of strikes against you. First of all, you're not married to this girl. Second, you don't even know where she is. Third, the laws of different states are not positioned to favor the father of the baby very much. Did you know that?"

"What do you mean?" Rafe asked.

"I mean that basically you don't exist in the eyes of the law," Henry said.

Rafe was stunned. He would never even have thought of any such issue. "That doesn't sound very hopeful."

"It's not," Henry said, "but if you'll let me continue looking at this a bit, I'll try to help you however I can."

Rafe continued sitting quietly for a minute. "Henry, how much do you think a thing like this might cost?"

"Depending on how far we are able to get, it could be very expensive." Henry sat back in his chair and put his fingertips together like Rafe had seen his father do so many times.

"I may not be able to go very far, Henry. I don't make a lot of money and my folks are not wealthy," Rafe said.

"What do you say we not talk money yet? I don't even know if I can help you." Henry saw a shadow pass over Rafe's face.

"Let's see what we can find out, and then I'll let you know what the cost is going to be," Henry added.

"Well, I know your hourly rate is more than I make an hour." Now Rafe smiled again. "You better keep a running tab and let me know before the pinball machine hits tilt, ok?"

"Will do. We call them 'billable hours.' You can bet I'll keep track. I don't want to give up my partner status just yet." Henry smiled, rose, and extended his hand again. "Keep your chin up, Rafe. It's a ragged road you're traveling, but let's see if we can smooth it out a bit. I'll call you when I have something. We've got your number on file?"

"Yes. I gave your receptionist my address and number. Thanks for taking this on." Rafe shook his hand and left.

Henry sat down in his chair and called Sally over the intercom again. "Sally, hold my calls, ok? And if Mrs. Samuels shows up, please ask her to wait for just a few minutes…keep her comfortable, will you?"

"Yes, Mr. Parker," came the reply.

Henry leaned his elbows on his desk and put his head in his hands. He had not felt so badly for a client in a long, long time.

16

It wasn't till late September that a shopping outing was arranged. Almost all the girls went on these outings, chaperoned by Miss Sullivan, a plain, slightly chubby woman whose actual age was difficult to determine. Rose was excited about getting away from 'campus' as Mrs. Kellogg called it. Going into town felt like a vacation. She and Liz talked about it on their way to breakfast.

"Thank heaven we're getting out of here for a while today," Rose began. "I can hardly wait to find some new clothes for you."

"You're not the only one. If I have to endure one more hateful stare or comment from Mrs. Kellogg, I'm likely to tell her to jump off the Empire State Building." It was clear Liz was in no mood for Mrs. Kellogg.

"I try to steer clear of her. Well, she hasn't said anything about your hair or makeup lately, right? That's something." Rose wanted to give her some encouragement. Liz had begun brushing her hair so that it framed her face more. She had stopped wearing eyeliner altogether for a while, but said it looked like her eyes were 'naked' and had begun wearing it again, applying only a fine line. She looked sort of like a pixie to Rose.

"She seems to seek me out," Liz said. "Like a tiger stalking her prey, right?"

They entered the dining room and sat down. Deeny was just a few seats down on the opposite side of the table. Deeny had made it clear that she did not like Liz, though there didn't seem to be any rational reason for it. She regularly made hateful remarks to or about Liz. Liz just blew it off most of the time.

"I see you're back to wearing your theater makeup," Deeny said to Liz. "You look like you belong in a strip club, if it wasn't for that huge stomach. Hard to entice any men with that basketball."

Liz didn't even look at Deeny, but Rose did. "What in the world is wrong with you, Deeny? Can we please just have a nice breakfast? We're all going away today. Let's make it a fun day."

At that, Liz did look up. "Rose, thank you, but you don't have to protect me. Deeny, you're a bitch, pure and simple. I know you don't like me, and I don't like you. You don't have to hang around with me, so why do you insist on dogging me? What have I ever done to you?"

Deeny's voice was full of disdain. "I just don't like the looks of you. You act ill-bred and wild. I can't believe they even let you in a place like this."

All the girls had stopped eating and were looking at each other, astonished about where this seemed to be heading - they didn't know if they should step in. One of Deeny's friends, Cindy, spoke up. "Come on, Deen...we don't want to do this today, right?"

Deeny appeared to not even have heard Cindy. "You look like you were raised in the street, or maybe in the jungle by wolves. I think you're a bad influence on Rose. You cuss like a sailor. You tell tales that just about make my hair curl. I don't think they should have let you in here. You're not a good person."

Liz rose from her seat, walked to Deeny's side of the table and stood over her, composed, but menacing. "We're all here for the same reason..." she said in a voice that was eerily calm. "We made a dumb mistake. But whoever knocked you up made the dumbest mistake of all."

Deeny jumped up and grabbed Liz's hair, screaming some unintelligible epithets. Liz fought right back, pulling Deeny's hair and swinging at Deeny, landing a blow wherever she could. The wait staff entered the room and pulled the two girls off each other, getting themselves roughed up a little in the process. By that time, one of the other girls had gone to get whatever administrator they could find, and lucky Dr. Pickens entered the room to see the girls being kept separated by women twice or three times their age.

"Ladies, ladies. Both of you in my office. Now." He turned and started walking towards the door. The girls followed, each escorted by one of the workers.

Rose didn't feel much like eating after the melee. She pushed her food around on her plate and prayed that Liz wouldn't be given restrictions that would prevent her from going on the shopping trip or worse yet, that the shopping trip would be canceled altogether.

She needed a day out of the home. They all did.

Rose walked up the steps to her room, just in time to see Alice getting ready to go downstairs, suitcase in hand. She had already delivered and was ready to leave Weingarten. Rose began to tear up.

"Oh, Alice, you dear girl. You were the first person who was kind to me here, and now you're going. I'm going to miss seeing you," Rose told her.

"I'll miss you, too, Rose, but I'm happy to be going home," Alice replied.

"Do you have time to sit and talk for a minute before you leave?" Rose asked.

Alice looked down at her watch. "Well, my parents aren't supposed to be here till 9, so I do have a little time. I was going to just wait in the sun room down by Mrs. Kellogg's office, but I may as well stay up here with you for a little bit."

They went into Rose's room and sat opposite each other in the chairs near the windows.

"Tell me what it was like," Rose began. "The labor and delivery, I mean. And what happens after the baby is born? Did you get to hold the baby?"

"Oh, heck no! I didn't even *want* to hold the baby!" Alice exclaimed. She dropped her eyes for a minute. "I think that holding the baby would make it really hard to let go of it again. I couldn't do it. And besides, they don't let you."

"Who doesn't let you?" Rose asked. She was surprised at this declaration.

"The doctor, the nurses, the social worker. Believe me, they're all right there. The nurses are taking care of the baby, of course – cleaning it up, making foot prints – all that sort of thing. But the social worker is right there too, waiting to get that kid handed over to its new parents." Alice was matter-of-fact about this part of the process.

"What about the labor and delivery?" Rose asked again.

"I don't know exactly what to say about that," Alice said. "I think it's probably a little different for everyone. For me, I knew I was going into labor because I had what they call a 'bloody show' and then my water broke. It was kind of a mess. After that, I pretty much stayed in bed and just tried to deal with the contractions. It was weird. I was very uncomfortable, especially my back. It was like a deep, deep pain that you couldn't get at. For me, it went pretty quick, though, so that was good."

"Did they give you any medicine for it?" Rose was hoping that would be the case.

"No, they actually didn't. They didn't want to hurt the baby's ability to breathe, they said. I just had to tough it out, but I did ok," Alice said with a shrug. Rose thought Alice seemed like a girl who would be 'ok' even if a bomb went off. In the months she had known her, Alice had always been a cool, calm, easy-going person.

"Well, I'm going to try hard to remember what you told me and not be scared," Rose said, "and I'll remember what a kind person you've been to me right from my first day in this place."

"Think nothing of it. When you come to a home like this, all you have is each other. I've got to go." Alice stood up and Rose stood up too...she wanted to give Alice a hug before she was gone forever.

"We'll never see each other again, so good-bye and good luck, Alice. You've been a peach," Rose said, wrapping her arms around her first friend at Weingarten.

"Good luck to you, too, Rose – trust me. You'll do just fine." Alice hugged her back and then pulled away, picked up her suitcase and turned to leave.

As she opened the door, Liz was on the other side, looking angry and defiant. When she saw Alice, she said, "Oh, good-bye you lucky thing. Get out of this looney bin while you can." She entered the room and flopped down on her bed.

Rose looked at Liz, then walked to the door. "Bye, Alice. Don't worry about us."

Alice walked towards the staircase, pausing at the top long enough to look at Rose one more time, giving her a little smile and a wave. Then she was gone.

"Good golly. What happened down there?" Rose closed the door to their room and sat in the chair closest to Lizzy's bed.

"That stupid bitch, Deeny, told Mrs. Kellogg that I started it by giving her a dirty look. Of course, Mrs. Kellogg believed her because, after all, I'm the evil one around here, right? I'm the troublemaker." Liz was clearly angry and discouraged at the same time.

"Did you get any restrictions?" Alice asked.

"She started to keep me from going shopping today, but I told her then she'd have to just deal with my clothing situation, so she changed her mind. However, I will be assigned extra chores – probably the ones that bitch Deeny is supposed to do. God, I hate that girl," Liz sputtered.

"Ok. I know you're mad as heck right now, but please, Lizzy…you've got to try to push it down, forget about it. We're going to get out of here today, and we can still have fun. We will just stay as far away from Deeny as possible and enjoy being free for a day." Rose was determined to make it a fun day, no matter what.

"Push it down. Is that what you do? Is that what you have to do so you don't think about Rafe and wanting to get married?" Liz knew immediately that she had jabbed her one and only real friend. She sat up on the side of the bed, seeing Rose's shocked, sad face.

"Rose, I'm so sorry. I didn't mean that. That was hateful. That was something like that stupid Deeny would say. Oh my God, I'm so sorry." Liz reached out her hands to Rose. "Please forgive me. You're one of the kindest people I've ever met. How could I say something like that to you? Rose, forgive me."

Rose already had. She squeezed both Liz' hands. "Listen to me, we've each had a day like this since we've been in here. Forget about it. You're my friend and we are going to have a great day together. Forget about Deeny. Forget about being mad. Let's start our day over and think about getting some new clothes and some ice cream. I want ice cream today, and doggone it, we're going to find someplace we can get some!" She smiled and stood up. "Come on. We don't want to miss the bus."

The girls grabbed their purses and headed downstairs. Deeny was in a group gabbing, not quite ready to board the bus. Liz and Rose moved themselves to a spot first in line so they could take the last seat on the bus and put space between them and Deeny. On the way downtown, Rose told Liz everything Alice had said about labor and delivery, about handing off the baby, about being excited about going home.

"I think she was smart to look at it all that way," Liz said when Rose had finished. "You can't get attached to these little beings or it will make it doubly hard to give them up. I really have no attachment to my baby…this baby was a complete accident. But you…you are in love with the father, and he's in love with you. That makes it torture to hand the baby over. How are you going to cope with all that?"

Rose sighed. "Well, they use all the brainwashing every week to get us ready for it, so maybe I'm starting to lose my attachment, too, I don't know. Let's not think about it today, ok? Let's just have fun."

They arrived downtown and before the girls disembarked, Miss Sullivan stood up at the front of the bus. "We are going to do something a little different today." She cleared her throat. "As you're all aware, we had a rough start to the morning." A few girls turned to look at Liz, but most everyone stared straight at Deeny, who maintained a look of innocence throughout Miss Sullivan's speech. "Mrs. Kellogg and I talked about it and thought that the close quarters you are always in may be contributing to overactive emotions. We decided that today you may all go shopping on your own. You must be with at least one other girl, but you do not all have to go to each store every other girl wants to go to. In other words, we don't travel as one big group today. You can go your own ways." At that, there was a great whoop from the entire bus.

"Let's you and I go by ourselves," Rose said to Liz. "Then we'll have plenty of space around us for a change and we can take all the time we need. Plus, we can find an ice cream stand."

Right then, Miss Sullivan added, "Make sure you are back at this location no later than 3 p.m. The bus will be leaving right at that time and will wait for no one. I assure you, it's a decently long walk for a pregnant girl, so you will not want to miss the bus."

Everyone stood up and crowded into the aisle. Liz and Rose stayed seated, waiting for the aisle to clear. Once most everyone was off the bus, they made their way to the front.

"Try to stay out of trouble, will you?" Miss Sullivan smiled, but she was serious.

"Don't worry about us. We'll be just fine," Rose said to her as they carefully made their way down the bus steps.

The two girls walked down the street, stopping to look in the occasional shop window; they noticed a store called MOMMY & BABY. They walked a block or so to the store's entrance and opened the door, arousing a few looks from the sales clerks.

"May I help you?" One clerk approached the girls, mannequin-like smile on her face.

"We're just looking around, but we may need you later," Rose said. The clerk went back to her work.

"This isn't my kind of place," Liz whispered, looking around. "I usually just shop at the thrift stores or the head shop."

"What's a head shop?" Rose asked.

Liz looked dumbfounded. "You know, where you buy bongs and pipes. They usually have some cool clothes, too."

"Bongs?" Rose asked.

"Oh my God, you're backwoods!" Liz laughed. "A bong! You know, for your weed!"

Rose glanced at the clerks to see if they had overheard this statement, then looked at Liz in disbelief. Lowering her voice to a whisper she said, "You know me well enough by now to know that I have never touched marijuana in my life and I probably never will. How in the world would I have known what a bong is?" Then she smiled. "You have lived a pretty daring life compared to me, my friend."

"Well, I can show you the ropes when we're not in prison anymore," Liz said, laughing. She knew Rose would never live a life like she had.

Rose stopped for a minute and said, "You know, we need to stop calling the home a prison. I mean, you actually paid your own money to live here and my father certainly probably paid through the nose. We have got to stop looking at it like a prison for our own mental health. Come on. We've got some clothes to buy."

The girls spent the better part of the afternoon picking out and trying on maternity tops and pants as well as dresses. They knew they had better be somewhat conservative or face the wrath of Mrs. Kellogg. After they had found some nice things and paid for them, they left, in search of treats to hide in their room.

They found a drug store where they could buy some snacks and hid the goodies in the bags with their clothes. They headed back outside into the bright sunlight.

"Ice cream." That was all Rose needed to say. Liz grabbed her arm and started down the street.

"I think I saw a little shop around the corner, not too far from where we got off the bus," Liz said, dragging Rose with her.

"Ok, ok, we don't have to run!" Rose cried, but both girls walked as quickly as they could.

"We probably look like a couple of pregnant dinosaurs trying to waddle along," Liz laughed.

"Speak for yourself!" Rose retorted.

Once inside the ice cream shop, they sat in wire-backed chairs while ceiling fans slowly rotated overhead. They looked at the ice cream flavors listed on a big board above the counter and debated about what would taste best on a hot day. Rose picked mint chocolate chip and Liz picked vanilla.

"Isn't that a little tame for such a wild woman?" Rose kidded her.

"Maybe so, but really, vanilla's my favorite," Liz answered.

When they were relaxing, enjoying the cool, creamy treats, Liz spoke up. "I can't tell you how much I appreciate you doing all this for me Rose. Just a month or so ago, we were total strangers. I've never met anyone as kind as you. Even my parents. Or Jimmy. If I believed in God, I'd tell him thanks."

"Don't even start this," Rose said. "I've been lucky in life. Luckier than most in a lot of ways. And Liz, I *do* believe in God and that there's a reason for everything. I don't think I would or could have accepted all this if I didn't believe in God. I'm not trying to tell you that you have to believe, too, but it's been about the only way I could face each day." She stopped for a minute. "That, and thinking about Rafe...I still believe he is trying to find me."

"I bet he is, too, if he has any sense...someone as wonderful as you...how could any guy stay away from you?" Liz seemed wistful. "I've never really known that kind of love, Rose. Except now, for you as my friend, anyway. Now I know a little more about love." She turned away, embarrassed by her own openness. "I don't usually get so mushy – I just think you're about the best person I ever met."

"Ha! If only you knew!" Rose laughed and hoped she could lift Lizzy's spirits.

"Oh yeah, like you're hiding some mean streak!" Liz laughed.

The girls sat and chatted and kidded back and forth for the rest of the afternoon. At 2:30, they walked back to the bus and were there in plenty of time. Deeny was already there, too, sitting on a bench at the bus stop. She shot Liz a contemptuous look. Liz and Rose hung back, waiting till the bus arrived to get any closer.

"No more repeats with that one," Liz said. "I'm not going to let her get under my skin anymore. I can't afford to have her chores added to mine every doggone week."

"Good thinking. I never liked her, either, Liz, not from day one, and it's definitely not worth it to tangle with her," Rose said quietly. "We'll just stick together. I can help you with your added chores this week."

"Oh, God no! After buying me all this stuff? No way. Besides, I can take it. I never let anything get me down for long," Liz replied.

"Well, that's good because we've still got plenty to get through," Rose said.

They boarded the bus. Tired, they sat quietly all the way home.

* * *

In another town, very far away from the subject of his search, Rafe Whitfield was also tired…tired of making visits to unwed mothers' homes across Chicago; tired of asking the same questions and getting the same answers. No one had ever heard of Rose Caswell, and even if they had, they wouldn't tell him. He had visited the Crittenden home and the Salvation Army home, as well as others that were not so famous. He was starting to give up on Chicago. His entire existence had become work, school, and his ongoing futile pursuit. Where else in this vast country could Rose be? Ham had done a superior job of sequestering her. His wealth had allowed him the benefit of secrecy. Rafe only hoped Henry Parker could help him….

17

The month of October passed exactly like all the other months had. Rose was happy to have Lizzy with her through the experience. Day in and day out, it was all the same, including Mrs. Kellogg's unpleasant dinners and disapproving stares. She really had it in for Liz, continuing to chide her about how she talked, how loud she laughed – whenever there was any opportunity for criticism, Mrs. Kellogg gladly delivered it.

They went to their regularly scheduled brow beatings with the psychologist. Dr. Pickens had decided Rose could come monthly but Lizzy was quite another matter – she had to continue weekly visits because of her "antisocial behavior," as Liz snickered on retelling the conversation.

The social worker persisted in preparing them for the eventual adoption of their babies. There was no other option ever discussed. Kathryn Baker laid it on thick every time Rose had to see her, which was also down to once a month. "Now you understand that our society simply does not accept illegitimate children. You'd never again have any respect, and your child would be subjected to the cruelest ridicule. You wouldn't want that. You'll be able to go to college - I'm sure your father will see to that – and you can get a fresh start. It's likely your hometown friends have figured out what happened to you. It's hard to keep this kind of thing secret, so you don't want to have to face that every day for the rest of your life. I actually recommend that you move to a new city when you've delivered and recovered."

The persistent haranguing started to take its toll on Rose, and she was beginning to think that maybe it really was for the best – giving up the baby. She didn't think about Rafe quite so often as she had when she first came to Weingarten. She had learned to push her feelings aside – it was too painful to think about what might have been. Even though it had only been a few months, it felt like Rafe had been part of her life a million years ago.

Her physician visits were going well – all was normal as could be. During her October appointment, Angie gave her some information about things she might experience as she went through her last month of pregnancy.

"Are you satisfied with my weight gain?" Rose asked Angie when they were back at the nursing station after the appointment. As of her eighth month, she had gained seventeen pounds.

"Yes, you're really right where you should be – you'll gain a few more pounds this next month. We like everyone to keep their weight gain to no more than 20 pounds. You're fine. But what in the heck is Lizzy doing?" Angie started laughing. "That girl has to be eating more than they give you at mealtime around here!"

Rose checked the hallway to make sure no one could overhear her. "We keep some snacks in our room. Please don't tell the doctor."

"I can assure you he's probably figured it out, Rose. Seriously, though, for Liz's sake, she needs to watch it. Everyone says that old thing about eating for two, but once that baby is born, you have to get all that weight back off and it's not so easy." Angie was pragmatic and matter-of-fact, always one to take a common-sense approach. "On top of that, extra weight does not help you during labor and delivery. It's just a fact."

"I'll try to keep her out of the Oreos every night," Rose smiled.

Angie laughed out loud. "Oh Lord. You girls! Maybe you can get her to eat an apple or an orange instead?"

"I doubt that – she'll probably choose *nothing* if she can't have Oreos. Thanks, Angie, I'll see you next month," Rose said.

"Oh, no, no - wait – you have to come weekly now. You're close enough to your due date that you must have a weekly visit. When you're having your first baby, the due date is a little less certain than if you've had other pregnancies. We're going to monitor your progress more closely, starting now. I'll see you next Wednesday at 10 a.m. Here's a card for you." Angie handed her an appointment card. Rose looked at it in disbelief. Was she really that close? It hardly seemed possible except for her growing stomach and the baby reminding her – the baby moved around all the time now.

Rose wrote letters to her father. She had to deliver them to Mrs. Kellogg, who was responsible for mailing them.

Liz asked her about it one day. "Gosh, do you ever get any letters back from your dad?"

"Well, not so far," Rose replied. "In a way I'm surprised, because as mad as he is at me, I believe he still loves me. I'll always be his little baby girl, you know? That's why he was so hurt, I suppose. Every time I write, I ask him to come get me, but as you see, here I still am."

"Well, at least you've got someone to write to, I guess," Liz answered.

And so the days went. Most of the girls in Cordelia Weingarten were forgotten souls, and they all knew it. There were rare visits from someone's parents; a reason for celebration for that girl...a sad reminder for all the others that they were outcasts.

Late in October during breakfast, Miss Sullivan came into the dining hall. She looked like she had good news.

"Girls, how would you all like to go to a movie?" she asked with a big smile on her face. The girls shouted unanimous approval for the idea, looking around, excited for an outing.

"I hear you, I hear you! Ok, we'll go to a movie. Now here's the next hurdle to overcome...what movie shall it be?" Miss Sullivan waited for suggestions.

"Well, what's playing?" a newcomer named Sue piped up. "We don't have a clue what movies are playing."

"I did bring the paper with me this morning...hold on and I'll get it," Miss Sullivan said. She left the room, and in her absence, excited chatter gave unusual life to what had started as a usual morning.

Miss Sullivan reappeared with a look of concern on her face as she folded and refolded the newspaper. "Well, ladies, I may have not picked the best time. The only movie that's playing right now is 'Rosemary's Baby.' I'm not so sure...."

She was interrupted by guffaws from all the girls. The very thought was so ludicrously perfect. Rosemary's Baby, indeed.

"I'm in!" Liz was the first to speak up. "Let's go see 'Rosemary's Baby.' It will be just like real life."

"Do you even know what 'Rosemary's Baby' is about?" Miss Sullivan asked. "I am not sure it's the kind of movie you ladies need to see right now. It's not a cheery motion picture. Have you read the book? Probably not. Maybe we should wait."

Outcries of protest arose.

"We want to go!"

"We're not scared."

"Come on, it's Halloween anyway!"

Miss Sullivan was frustrated. "Oh bother! All right then. If you all have nightmares, it's your own fault. The bus will be here at 7 p.m. because the movie starts at 7:35. If you're not in the lobby on time, you're out of luck. And God help us if the movie scares the bejeebers out of you. You know, people sometimes go into early labor from a big fright such as you might get in the movies."

The girls guffawed again at this old wives' tale.

"Go on with you, then," Miss Sullivan admonished. "I've given you all fair warning."

Liz and Rose went to their room, eager for another adventure away from the home. They went through their day whistling, singing, and smiling. Even Deeny was in a chipper mood.

The girls hardly ate their dinner that night – they were too excited.

"I'm having a large popcorn, anyway," Liz told Rose. "That is, if you're buying."

"I'll bring the checkbook," Rose kidded her.

At the appointed time, they all loaded into the bus and went to the Apple Blossom Theater. It was an older theater in the heart of the downtown area, not far from where Liz and Rose had enjoyed ice cream on a warmer day.

The movie was everything the girls' minds could take in. From the creepy opening music to the final credits, Rose shivered in the dark, and occasionally, Liz squeezed her arm in shock or fright...Rose wasn't sure which. Throughout the movie, they heard gasps and groans from other movie goers. Rose had to muffle a laugh when she heard one older lady cry out loud, "Don't look in there!"

When the movie was over, the girls all stood. Miss Sullivan was at the end of the row nearest the aisle, and she wasted no time in heading up the aisle for the door of the theater. Liz grabbed Rose's arm.

"Look," she hissed. "Exit."

Rose turned to see what Liz was pointing at. There was a red neon EXIT sign near the movie screen.

"Yeah...so what?" Rose asked.

Liz began pulling her out the other end of the row of seats. "Let's go! Hurry!"

Rose followed along, not that she had much choice. Liz had a death grip on her arm.

"Where are we going?" Rose asked. "We'll miss the bus."

"Don't worry. We'll find a ride home. Come on!" Liz insisted.

Rose was hesitant, but didn't want Liz out running around town on her own. Liz was brave - just a little too brave, maybe.

They snuck out the back of the theater. They were in an alley, with the backs of stores facing them. The Cigar Room. Staley's Dry Goods & Sundries. The Tap Room.

"Here, this is the one," Liz said as she opened the back door to The Tap Room. She pulled Rose inside.

"Lizzy, you know we shouldn't be in a place like this," Rose pleaded. "Mrs. Kellogg already has it in for you…you're just inviting more trouble. Come on, now. If we hurry, maybe we can still catch the bus."

"Chicken. Hey, one of these guys will get us home. I'm not even worried." Liz was resolute.

"Well, I'm not paying for a bunch of beer," Rose said.

"Don't worry. We won't pay for even one," Liz winked.

They sat down at the bar. Rose looked around at the other patrons. She had never been in a place like this in all her time in Kinston. There were bars in Kinston, but she had never been in one. She had heard Stuart talk about the bars he frequented. She didn't like how Stu came home from those bars, usually disheveled and smelling of beer or whiskey and cigarettes.

Liz spoke to a man who was sitting next to her. "Hi there. What are you doing in here alone, you handsome devil?"

The man turned to face her. He was anything but handsome. He was unshaven, unsmiling, with a cigarette hanging out of his mouth where a tooth should have been. His bulbous nose was blood red.

"I ain't alone. I'm here with my one and only friend, Jim Beam." He laughed loudly at his own joke, and Liz laughed loudly too, encouraging him.

"Well, I wouldn't mind meeting your friend Jim Beam," Liz said. "He sounds like a real nice fellow."

The older gentleman now turned on his bar stool to look at her more carefully. He peered at her for a long time through watery blue eyes, swaying a little bit as he looked her up and down.

"Are you sure you ought to be meeting up with a fellow like Jim?"

he asked. "You look like you mighta already met a fellow."

"Yeah, well, I did and now he's gone, so…I'm ready to meet someone new." Liz poured it on. It wasn't long before the bartender approached Liz and Rose.

"Ladies, what can I get you? This gentleman is buying you both a round."

Liz spoke up first. "Hey, I'll just have a draft beer."

The bartender looked at Rose. "You?"

"I'll have a Dr. Pepper," Rose replied.

"Wow, you're going for the hard stuff," Liz snorted.

"I've never been much of a drinker. I've seen too much at home. Plus it's bad for the baby. I'll stick with soda," Rose replied.

"You act like you still think that baby is yours," Liz said sarcastically, but she soon reverted back into her charming self.

Liz hadn't been fooling about not paying for drinks. She worked the room like a politician, slapping backs and chatting people up, just like Rose had seen her father do so many times. Rose stayed seated at the bar. She felt like it was safer, somehow. Liz flitted through the crowd like she was among old friends, talking and laughing with everyone she met. Eventually, Rose knew they needed to be concerned about the hour - the front doors of the home locked at 10 p.m. sharp. She carefully slipped down off her barstool and walked over to Liz, who was sitting at a table with a group of older women.

"Yeah, my old man left me," Rose heard Liz saying as she approached. "It's all right. He wouldn't have been much of an addition to the family." She laughed bitterly when she said it, and Rose knew now that Liz had been drinking just a little too much.

"Come on, Liz. We've got to get going. We're going to be in a world of trouble," she whispered in Liz's ear.

Liz stood up, hearing the firmness of Rose's demand. "Nice to meet you ladies. Thanks for the beer."

Rose took Liz by the arm now and walked out the front door. It was dark and the streetlights were on. It was also chilly, and they only had sweaters.

"How will we get back by 10 o'clock?" Rose said to no one. Liz wasn't even paying attention, unconcerned, thanks to the beer.

"We're in deep shit, aren't we?" Liz finally said, slurring a little.

"I would say that's an accurate assessment," Rose replied. "How did I let you get me into this?" Then she chuckled. "Liz, you're more trouble and more fun than anyone I ever knew. Come on, you idiot. We've got to get walking. Straighten up. You're in for a hike."

She paused and thought for a second. Rose had paid attention on the group trips downtown and had a good sense of direction. She knew how to get them home, but they walked forever, it seemed.

When they finally got to Weingarten, the house was very dark. The only light that was on was in the foyer. They walked up to the door and tried the knob. It was locked.

Rose looked at Liz. She was more alert now that she had walked a good part of the beer out of her system, but it was clear she was tired. So was Rose.

"Now what?" Liz asked.

Just then, the heavy door swung open and Miss Sullivan stepped out onto the porch.

"Welcome ladies. So good of you to finally join us." Her tone was stinging, sarcastic.

"We're sorry Miss Sullivan. We really are. We just wanted to walk around downtown a little bit and we got lost. Then we couldn't get back to the bus in time. We tried to find a Good Samaritan to help us out, but..." Rose began to fib.

"Save it!" Miss Sullivan now shouted. "Save it for Mrs. Kellogg! Do you two know you nearly cost me my job tonight? I got a routing from Mrs. Kellogg the likes of which I've never heard! I just about got sacked. I had to beg her to keep me on. Don't give me your sob story. Just get in here and get yourselves up to bed. Mrs. Kellogg will deal with you both in the morning."

The girls walked into the foyer. They both felt terrible. Besides the nurses, Miss Sullivan was one of the few at the home who ever showed any compassion whatsoever.

"I'm sorry, Miss Sullivan," Liz said. "I kind of made Rose go along with me. It was all my idea."

"That doesn't surprise me one bit. You both smell like a tavern. I'd advise you to get upstairs and shower, and wash your hair. Otherwise you'll smell like cigar smoke when you have to face Mrs. Kellogg in the morning."

It was a fitful night for Rose, but Liz slept like the dead, no doubt because of the beer she had consumed. Rose wondered what it would do to Liz's weight. She was scheduled for her doctor appointment in the afternoon.

Rose had difficulty getting Liz awake the next day. Liz rolled over a couple of times and opened her eyes and then closed them again, muttering, "I don't feel good. Let me sleep. I don't want any breakfast." She finally got up just in time to make it to breakfast, but all she had was a couple of bites of toast and a cup of coffee. Rose was concerned. Liz looked more pale and washed out than she should have been for the amount she had drunk. But what did Rose know about it? All she ever saw at home was her father, who could drink like a fish and still function, or Stuart, who was a sloppy drunk. Two grown men on opposite ends of the spectrum. Maybe Liz would feel better later, but she knew they had to face Mrs. Kellogg. She was not looking forward to it.

Mrs. Kellogg was waiting for them both right outside the dining hall.

"Elizabeth, I'll see you first. Rose, you may wait in the sitting room." Her voice was controlled but ugly - low and alarming.

Rose watched as Liz disappeared into Mrs. Kellogg's office, then went to the sitting room. The sky was gray. She *felt* gray. She didn't hear a sound from the office and prayed that it was going easy for Lizzy.

After a time, Liz appeared but never even looked at Rose. She headed up the grand staircase where Rose had once pictured debutantes. Lizzy's head was bowed – a vision of a scullery maid who had been beaten by her master.

"Rose…" Mrs. Kellogg beckoned.

Rose entered the office and did not wait to be invited before sitting down. She was still tired from her long walk last night and she didn't even care if Mrs. Kellogg was a grouch that morning. She was just too tired to worry about it.

"How you could let yourself be lead into such hijinks as you committed last night is a mystery to me, Rose. You surely know better." Mrs. Kellogg's voice was as cold as a January midnight. "I do everything I can to make this a good environment for you girls – we keep you safe, we keep you healthy, we keep you busy so that you don't ruminate over your situation. We provide medical care, education, psychological and social assistance. I don't know why you and Elizabeth are so ungrateful for all this, because that's what your choice last night indicates. That you are both ungrateful and immature."

Rose tried to interrupt her, but Mrs. Kellogg put a hand up and went on. "You are both confined to the house for the duration of your pregnancy. You will be assigned additional chores. You will both see Dr. Pickens each week. He may decide that you need some behavior-modifying medication, I don't know. What I do know is that we are going to get you through this pregnancy and as soon as you are fully recovered, you will be going back home. There is nothing else to be said at this time. You may return to your room now."

Rose got up, started to say something, but saw that Mrs. Kellogg had turned her back and was intent on some papers in her hand. She left.

Back in her room, she looked at her chore schedule. Linen room. That was a good chore – clean environment, not so much stooping, bending, or kneeling. She didn't know what Liz had on the schedule today, so she walked over to Liz' makeshift desk (a box set up on one end) and looked. SCRUB KITCHEN AND DINING ROOM FLOORS. Rose was shocked. Would they really have Liz mopping floors when she was as far along as she was? That was a job generally assigned girls who were early in their pregnancy. The linen room would have to wait. She went to find Liz.

She went to the dining room first. It was already spotless, so she knew Liz must be in the back, mopping the kitchen. She pushed open the swinging door and entered, finding Liz alone, on her knees with a bucket of soapy water and a sponge. Rose gasped at the sight.

"Gees, you scared the crap out of me!" Liz cried. "What the heck are you doing in here?"

"Looking for you, you big ninny. What in God's name are you doing on your knees? Why aren't you using the mop?" Rose replied. "Are you crazy? You're eight months pregnant!"

"Tell it to good old Mrs. Kellogg. She's the one who told me the floor needed to be hand-scrubbed today. I really don't feel well, so after she left I looked all over for the mop but I'll be damned if I could find one." Liz was a little out of breath while she talked.

"That old bat probably hid it!" Rose was so angry she was shaking. "I'll find that mop!"

Rose stormed out and went directly to Mrs. Kellogg's office. She knocked, then opened the door without waiting for a response. Mrs. Kellogg was talking on the phone. "I'll call you back in just a minute," she said into the receiver, giving Rose a withering stare.

"What is the meaning of this?" Mrs. Kellogg spit out. "What on earth are you thinking, barging into my office this way?"

"Mrs. Kellogg, what would ever possess someone to make a pregnant girl – eight months pregnant, mind you – scrub a filthy, greasy kitchen floor on her hands and knees? This is outrageous, even for you. I've kept my mouth shut about a lot of things around here, especially about how you treat Elizabeth, but I'll stay silent no longer. How could you?" Rose caught her breath.

"How dare you?" Mrs. Kellogg came right back at her. "You are not in charge here. You do not make the rules, you *follow* the rules, and the same goes for your trouble-making friend, Elizabeth. Now get out!"

Rose summoned every bit of strength she could pull out of her normally timid character. "You had best tell me where the mop is right now or I'll tear this place apart finding it! What's more, when I get out of here, don't think I won't tell my father about this."

Mrs. Kellogg narrowed her eyes, sneered, and hissed, "And what exactly do you think your rich father will do about anything? Do you really expect that he will want his friends to know that he has any affiliation with this place? He would never speak of it in decent society."

Rose winced. Mrs. Kellogg was right, and now she came in for the kill. "Despite all your letters, your precious father's never even been here to see you. None of your family has been here to see you and that supposed boyfriend of yours hasn't either. So don't tell me what you'll do. You'll do what I tell you to do."

Rose looked at the twisted, angry face in front of her and realized that she couldn't win against this woman, possessed of hate and evil as she seemed to be.

"You're right, Mrs. Kellogg," Rose said quietly. "You're right, as usual. We pregnant girls really have no one, do we? Not even you. For all your Christian pretense, you really don't give a hoot about a single soul here. How do you think the God you pray to would feel about that? Look in the mirror, Mrs. Kellogg, before you get down on your knees next time. Maybe you should think about what it is your God wants you to do for the girls who live here. Love. Forgiveness. I seem to remember that from my lessons at Sunday school. What did you learn at your church?"

Rose left, but not before Mrs. Kellogg muttered "whores" under her breath.

She went back to the kitchen and found Liz taking a little break. She was still short of breath and sweating now, too. "Are you all right, Lizzy?" Rose asked. "I can't find the doggone mop, but I'm going to help you get this floor done."

"No, I'm basically done with it. I just needed to get my breath before I try to stand up," Liz replied.

They waited a few minutes with Liz in a sitting position, back up against the oversized refrigerator. Rose put away the bucket and sponge and waited for Liz to give a signal that she was ready to go back to their room.

"Rosie Posey, I've got to get up. Will you help me?" Liz said.

"Of course," said Rose, hurrying over to help her.

When she was halfway to her feet, Liz cried out in pain. "Oh my God, that hurt! I must be going into labor."

"Oh Lizzy! Oh Lord! Let's get you right upstairs. Can you walk? Should I get someone?" Rose asked, anxious.

"Who would you get? Mrs. Kellogg? Fat lot of help she would be," Liz said sarcastically. "No, I can make it if you just help me."

The two pregnant girls made their way up the steps slowly, with several stops along the way as Liz doubled over in pain.

"I thought they said it doesn't really hurt," Liz complained. "I thought they said it just feels 'uncomfortable'."

"They tell us that so we won't be so scared when it starts," Rose said. "You know that. Come on, let's get you into bed and then I'll go get Deb or Angie."

They made it to their room, and Liz practically dropped onto the bed. "Rose, I really don't feel good. I mean, I feel real weird."

"I'll be right back," Rose said. She threw a coverlet from her own bed over her friend and practically ran up the steps to the third floor.

"Deb? Angie? Who's here today?" Rose knew she sounded panicked, running down the hall and calling out as she was.

Angie stepped out of an exam room into the hall. Seeing Rose, she looked alarmed. "Rose honey, what's wrong?"

"I think Liz is in labor. She's having pains off and on."

"Did her water break or anything like that?" Angie asked. "Are the pains frequent? Are they even regular yet?"

Rose thought for a second. "Well, her water didn't break, I know that much. I didn't time her pains, but when we were coming up the steps, she had to stop two – no, three times. She was doubled over, it hurt so bad."

At the words "doubled over," a look of concern crossed Angie's face.

"Rose, listen to me. We're getting ready to deliver Deeny up here. Dr. Oppenheimer's over in the delivery room right now. What's more, we think she's going to have twins…we're not sure yet. In any event, we've got our hands full. June Weston is in the delivery room with Dr. Oppenheimer and I'm finishing up with this patient. I'm going to call Deb to come in because we're getting in over our heads now. I want you to do this for me. Go back and stay with Liz. Take your watch and time how frequent her contractions are. Keep track of it for me, ok? I've got to run in and help with Deeny's babies, but I'll be there in just a few minutes, ok? Can you do that for me?"

"Sure. Please hurry as much as you can," Rose said over her shoulder. She was already on her way back down to her friend.

In their room, Liz was lying on her side, now, facing the door. "Gees, Rosie, my back is killing me. It hurts like hell. And I'm having contractions pretty often. I feel like I have to go to the bathroom, but I'm scared I'll pass out if I get up. Will you help me?"

Rose noticed that Lizzy was pale, breathing fast. "Lizzy, I'm not sure you *should* get up." Rose walked over to the bed.

"I have to, Rose, or I'll pee myself." Liz tried to sit up, and Rose offered her arm, trying to help Liz up. "I'll just go to the bathroom and then come right back to bed. Oh, criminy, I'm nauseated, too."

They waited a few seconds, then Liz said, "Let's go." She stood up and took a couple of steps, Rose holding on to her arm.

"Uh-oh, Rose. I think my water just broke," Liz said.

Rose looked down. What she saw scared her beyond any ability to speak. Bright red blood was running down Lizzy's legs. It was like nothing Rose had ever seen coming out of a human, not even when she was on her period, and she knew it was not at all normal. She felt frozen with fear for a minute, then Liz seemed to be passing out. She urinated on the floor and started to fall. Rose eased her down to the floor and ran to the door.

"Help, help!" she screamed as loudly as she could into the empty hall. "Get the nurses! Get Mrs. Kellogg!"

Rose hurried back over to Liz's side, trying to rouse her. "Lizzy, wake up! Lizzy, open your eyes!"

One of the girls, Pamela, walked into the room with Mrs. Kellogg in tow. They both looked at Liz and Rose, mouths open.

"Go get a nurse," hissed Mrs. Kellogg. Pamela immediately left the room.

"Mrs. Kellogg, help me get her in bed," Rose pleaded. "I think she's dying."

"Don't be ridiculous. She's just had her bloody show," Mrs. Kellogg barked.

"Do you pass out with a bloody show?" screamed Rose. She turned back to Liz. "Liz, can you hear me? Wake up. We've got to get you back in bed."

Liz moaned and grimaced as if she were in pain. Rose could see that her abdomen was contracting hard and fast.

"Mrs. Kellogg, help me!" Rose screamed again.

The sound of Rose's panicked voice seemed to motivate Mrs. Kellogg to action. The two women picked Liz up as best they could and half dragging her, got her placed on the bed. Now all the blood that had been pouring out of Liz was on the floor, staining the rose-patterned rug a bright scarlet.

Mrs. Kellogg's eyes opened wide, and her mouth dropped open. She gasped and said, "I'll go find the nurse myself. Stay right with her." She didn't run, but she was moving very fast.

Rose saw a crowd of girls huddling together in the hall outside their room. "Help us or get away!" she screamed at them, and they scattered like a herd of frightened deer.

Rose turned to Liz. "Liz, open your eyes, listen to my voice. It's Rose. My darling friend, please open your eyes."

Liz seemed to come to for a minute, trying to obey Rose's command, but she could barely open her eyes, showing only a glimpse of the green light that Rose had come to love.

"Rose? Rose?" Liz said, too weak to speak above a whisper.

"I'm right here. The nurses are on the way. Hang on. I think you're having the baby." Rose knew there was more than that going on, but she was trying to reassure her friend and maybe convince herself, too. She tried to push away her fear and concentrate on Liz.

The door banged open and Angie appeared. "Dear Jesus!" she uttered, noticing the blood all over the floor. She turned back to Mrs.

Kellogg. "Go up to the nurse's station, get on the intercom into the delivery room and tell Deb and Dr. Oppenheimer that they need to get down here as soon as possible – STAT!" Mrs. Kellogg disappeared, now clearly concerned about the unfolding events.

Angie came to Liz's bedside. "Liz...Liz, can you hear me? I'm going to check your blood pressure." Angie first felt for a pulse and had a hard time finding it. "Rose, you better start moving some furniture away from that door and get one of the other girls or someone downstairs to call the hospital and have them send an ambulance. This is an emergency and we can't handle this kind of situation here."

Rose moved Liz's funny desk and a floor lamp. She tried to make sure there was a clear path to the bed.

Suddenly, Liz screamed out. Angie was pulling back her hand from Liz's abdomen. "Oh Rose, we don't have time. This is bad. Go find someone to call that ambulance, and tell them to hurry it up."

Rose was just stepping into the hall when Deb and Mrs. Kellogg showed up. They walked into the room and found Angie pumping up the blood pressure cuff. Rose said, "I'm going to call the ambulance."

Mrs. Kellogg said, "I'll do that. You stay here." Once again, she disappeared from the chaos.

Deb had brought the medical supply bag with her and was putting an intravenous in Lizzy's hand. Liz was thrashing around a bit, making it hard for Deb. Rose went to her bedside and tried to calm Liz down. "Talk to her Rose," Deb instructed her.

"Lizzy, remember when we went shopping, the fun we had? Remember that yummy ice cream we had afterwards?" Rose was crying, trying to keep her voice from quavering. She wanted to be as effective in helping Liz as the nurses who were working on her. They seemed to have nerves of steel in all this chaos.

"Rose, hold her hand for me," Deb said. "I've got the needle in but I've got to tape it so it doesn't come out and she's still too wiggly." Rose did as she was told.

"Liz, open your eyes. Talk to me. Stay with me," Rose implored, holding the arm as tightly as she could while Deb taped the intravenous into place and made the fluid run into Liz's vein very fast.

"I've got to check the bleeding," Angie said. She lifted the covers. Blood was everywhere, soaking into the bed linens and continuing to ooze down two very pale legs. Clots were beginning to form. To Rose, it looked like Liz had been shot. Angie and Deb looked at each other, grim-faced. They continued their ministrations, as best they could, while Rose held Liz's hand.

Liz suddenly gave out a great cry, startling the three women at her bedside. "Don't let me die!"

Now Rose cried in earnest. She smoothed Liz's hair, stroked her cheek and continued to talk into Liz's ear. "Liz, Lizzy, don't give up. Stay with us. I need you." But Liz barely responded. Then she opened her eyes, wide and wild, looking around the room for something she couldn't seem to find. She turned her gaze slowly to Rose and whispered, "Eberly. My last name is Eberly." Her voice was quiet and clear as a bell. Just as suddenly, she closed her eyes and her head collapsed to one side.

"Deb, I can't feel a pulse, can you?" Angie asked quietly, her fingers over Liz's carotid.

Deb checked Liz's wrist, then along the opposite carotid.

"No, I can't," Deb replied.

"We've got to do CPR." The two nurses began pushing on Liz's chest and blowing breaths into her mouth. Rose had never seen such a thing, and she backed up, stumbling over something in the floor. She fell, putting her hand down in the blood on the rug. She raised her hand to her face and looked at it, horrified, and got up as fast as she could. The scene was too much. Rose began to crumple onto her own bed. She didn't even realize she was screaming until Mrs. Kellogg came back into the room and shook her like a rag doll.

"Shut up! Shut up, you idiot! You're not helping anything! Stop this screaming!" Mrs. Kellogg was screaming herself.

The nurses kept working but in between breaths, Deb calmly said, "Mrs. Kellogg, your screaming is not helping, either." Mrs. Kellogg bristled, but moved away from Rose, who now whimpered into her pillow. She could not watch any more.

The nurses kept at the CPR, and finally Dr. Oppenheimer showed up. "Good God. What do we have? An abruption?" He looked at the blood all around Liz and said, "Girls, stop CPR for a minute. Do you even have a pulse?"

Both nurses reached for a wrist, then the carotid area.

"No sir. I think she's gone." Angie spoke up, genuine sadness in her tone.

"Is an ambulance on the way?" the physician asked.

"Yes, I expect to hear the siren any second," Mrs. Kellogg said, and as if right on cue, a distant wailing got closer, closer, and then finally stopped. They could hear a racket coming up from the foyer; attendants with a stretcher appeared at the door.

"I'm afraid you're too late, chaps," Dr. Oppenheimer said, "but she'll need to go to the hospital anyway for pronouncing. And I suppose they'll want an autopsy." He started for the door, saying to Mrs. Kellogg "I've got paper work to fill out, then I'll go 'round and speak to the coroner."

That was it. Liz was gone. Mrs. Kellogg was following the physician out of the room like his shadow. The nurses began cleaning up. Rose was suddenly filled with a blind rage. She jumped up from her bed and followed Mrs. Kellogg and Dr. Oppenheimer out into the hall.

"Where were you? Why didn't you come when she needed you? You quack! You may just as well have killed her!" Rose was flailing her fists at Dr. Oppenheimer, and Mrs. Kellogg was trying without much success to stop her. "And you!" she continued, striking at Mrs. Kellogg. "You did this! You did this to her!"

"Rose, stop it! Stop it!" Angie appeared in the hall and tried to pull Rose away from the stunned doctor and administrator. Once again, a crowd of pregnant girls had gathered in the hall, mouths gaping.

Rose stopped and looked at Angie, then at the other girls, and at that moment every bit of pain and sorrow she had carried for the last five months fell on her like a millstone. She was crushed under the weight of it all and sank down to the floor, sobbing.

"Liz, oh, Liz," she cried. "My friend...."

"Give her a dose of Valium," Rose heard the doctor say. "Five milligrams ought to be enough. Give it intramuscular."

Angie helped Rose to stand and said, "Come with me, Rose. Let me help you now. You'll be all right in a little bit. Let me help you," and she lead Rose to the elevator that said TO LABOR AND DELIVERY ROOMS ONLY. "We're going to take the elevator today. It will be all right."

"Who's with Liz? Who's helping Liz?" Rose suddenly became agitated, trying to pull away to go back to her friend.

"Deb is with Liz, don't you worry. You know Deb will take good care of Lizzy," Angie reassured her, urging her towards the elevator.

Rose let Angie lead her. She was too shaky to do anything else. Her friend was gone, the baby would never meet its new parents. She cried now, without making a sound as Angie, also in tears, held her hand.

Elizabeth Eberly was dead.

18

In the days after Liz's death, Rose knew she wasn't coping well, but she couldn't seem to pull herself out of it. She didn't really sleep, tossing and turning fitfully every night, thinking about Liz, missing and crying for her friend, wondering if she could potentially share the same fate. The dark circles under Rose's eyes reappeared for good.

The maintenance men had come and removed Liz's bed and most of her belongings. The cleaning staff had tried to take the rug with Liz's blood stain from the room, but Rose screamed at them to leave it alone, telling them it was the only part of her friend she had left. They looked at her horrified, like she was a lunatic, but she didn't care. She wanted it there. It was a grim reminder.

She started wearing some of the clothes she had bought for Liz. Her friend was dead, but wearing her clothes kept her memory close, more alive. Rose stopped wearing makeup or doing anything much to her hair. It really didn't matter to her anymore.

She showed up for meals, but she barely ate and started losing weight. Her arms and legs were too thin; her face became gaunt.

Angie and Deb were worried, and even Dr. Oppenheimer seemed concerned. He tried to talk to Rose about Liz's circumstances, reassure Rose that what happened to Liz was rare.

"Your friend had an abruptio placentae," the doctor told Rose. "In other words, her placenta started tearing off the wall of her uterus. In Elizabeth's case, it tore quickly and she bled out. I should say she hemorrhaged to death. We just don't have the kind of environment where we can take care of an emergency like that. We try our best, but usually, we get these girls to the hospital before...well, before they die like Elizabeth did. This kind of situation has been so rare here at Weingarten that I'd have to go back years to even find another case. That's what I want you to know about all this, Rose – it's very rare. Even out in the wide world, it's not common. I'm quite certain you will not suffer such an outcome, and I'm truly sorry your friend died."

Rose stared blankly, looking back and forth between the doctor and Angie. Finally, she spoke.

"What about the babies? They die with the mother. Do they just have one funeral? What about the parents who were going to adopt that baby? Did they go to the funeral? Who was there for Lizzy?" Rose was staring at the wall behind him now, emotionless.

The line of questioning was so startling to the physician that he said, "Rose, give me a minute. I will be right back. You just wait here, all right?" He left the room, taking Angie with him.

"I'm afraid this girl is losing her mind," Dr. Oppenheimer started. "I'm very worried about her ability to get through labor and delivery when she's in a state like this. I'm thinking we should probably plan for her to deliver at the hospital. She may need more than we can give her here."

"Dr. O," Angie responded, "Rose has been through a lot. Of course, *all* these girls go through a lot, but Rose...here's the thing...I'm afraid that going out of this environment may make things worse for her. I think Elizabeth was really her only good friend, but she does have me and Deb. She trusts us and relies on us. You know Deb and I don't get too emotionally involved most of the time – we always try to keep it friendly, but professional. These young pregnant women need that. But Rose has been different. Her situation has just seemed all the sadder because it really does appear that she's being forced to give up this child. I don't know...I just hate to see her go to the hospital."

"One thing I learned in medical school was to listen to the nurses," Dr. Oppenheimer said. "For one thing, if you don't listen, they'll bug you till you do." He looked over his glasses and smiled. "You know I'm kidding you a bit, right? But seriously, I do think nurses tend to have their finger right on the patient's pulse, if you'll pardon the pun. If you think we'd be better off to have her stay, that's what we'll do. The pregnancy itself is quite normal and I'm not concerned about any risk as far as that goes. Just the same, I'm going to talk to Pickens again. Rose may need some medication to lift her spirits. That's an area I'm not familiar with. I'll stick with obstetrics. Let's go back in to her."

They went back in to the exam room. They found Rose shredding a cotton ball she had pulled out of a glass jar. The jar's metal lid was still off and cotton balls were strewn over the top of the stand.

"What are you doing Rose?" Angie asked.

"Thinking about home. Wesley and the other men have all the cotton off and to market by now." Rose's voice was quiet. She seemed distant, distracted.

Angie looked at the doctor and whispered, "I'll watch out for her, I promise." She put her arm around Rose's shoulder. "Rose, let's get you back to your room now."

The two women left the exam room, and Dr. Oppenheimer, shaking his head, sat down to make notes about his concerns. He was determined to talk to Dr. Pickens and Mrs. Kellogg that day.

Back in Rose's room, Angie thought she might be able to get through to Rose – snap her back to reality - by simply being blunt. She sat down across the room from the pale, thin girl.

"Rose, your baby is ok right now, but it won't be if you don't pull yourself out of this funk you're in. I don't want to sound mean, but you've got to snap out of this. Listen, I shouldn't tell you this, but Dr. Oppenheimer is ready to send you to the hospital to deliver. You won't have me or Deb with you if that happens. I know you're sad, but you have got to get your head clear. Do you hear what I'm saying? Do you understand me? Your baby will suffer if you don't start eating and taking better care of yourself. Rose, do you want Rafe's baby to suffer?"

At the invocation of Rafe's name, Rose's head shot up, and she shook it as if to clear a fog.

"No. I don't want the baby to suffer," Rose said, but her tone was flat. Angie was still worried.

"Then you've got to pull yourself together, Rose. I can't do it for you. Deb can't do it for you. *No one* can do it for you. You've got to do it for yourself and your baby. You can't help Liz now. We're all sad and horrified that she died right here – God help us, we're just minutes away from a hospital - but she's dead and you're alive. You can't blame yourself, you can't blame anyone – it was a freak situation that killed her, and now you've got to pick yourself up and carry on for the sake of your own child. The baby inside *you* needs a healthy mother, too."

"Yes, of course...you're right. I've got to take care of myself. I will. I'll do that." She looked at Angie. "Don't worry. I'll do better now."

Angie wasn't convinced, but patted Rose on the shoulder and said, "That's my girl." She had trouble controlling her own tears. Some people just have too much to bear, Angie thought as she closed the door behind her.

Angie went with Dr. Oppenheimer to talk to Mrs. Kellogg, Dr. Pickens, and Kathryn Baker about Rose's depression in a group conference. No one seemed concerned that Rose had become a ghost of herself.

"If you're insistent upon it, I could offer some mood elevators to help bring her out of it," Dr. Pickens said, "but you have to consider the effect on the fetus."

"I could try to assign her another roommate," Mrs. Kellogg offered, thinking it wouldn't hurt if she could increase revenue for the home.

"I can't really back off my adoption preparation," Kathryn said.

The doctor and nurse looked at each other. They were wasting their breath. "We'll keep an eye on her," Dr. Oppenheimer said. He and Angie left. "Talking to that group is like talking to a wall," he said. "Well, Angie, we've had some challenges before. Miss Rose Caswell is our next, I guess."

* * *

Rose got up too late for breakfast the next day. She had promised Angie she'd do better, so she took a cookie out of her snack drawer and nibbled, though she nearly choked on it. She was due to see Kathryn Baker that morning. She had decided to sign the adoption papers. She couldn't care for a baby – she knew that now. She could barely care for herself.

She got ready to take a shower, looking for a minute at herself in the mirror. She was due at any time. Her stomach was huge, looking even larger because her arms and legs were so thin now. She got into the shower and stood under the hot water, letting it wake her up.

It won't be long now. I'll finally go home.

She got dressed. When she walked out of her room, she found a reminder on her door about her meeting with Kathryn Baker. She looked for her chore list and saw that she had none. Instead, she was scheduled to meet with Mrs. Kellogg and Dr. Pickens.

Kathryn Baker had never been unkind to her, exactly, but she was always very focused on getting adoption arrangements completed.

On this day, Rose made it easy for her.

"What all do I have to sign to give my baby away?" Rose asked, looking down at her hands.

Kathryn was shocked. All along, Rose had insisted that her boyfriend would be here for her eventually, that she wanted to keep her baby.

"Well, I can't say I'm not happy about your change of attitude about this, but I'm surprised. What has caused you to rethink adoption?" Kathryn gloated to herself, thinking her own role in their weekly visits had changed the girl's mind at last.

"I don't know. I just give up, I guess." Rose continued to look at her hands, seeming to be engrossed in her fingernails.

"Good. We can get this finished up today. Once the baby is delivered, it will be given to the next family on the waiting list. Rose, you do understand that once you've made this decision, there's no going back. Once you sign the papers, the baby you are carrying is no longer yours." Kathryn leaned across her desk. "Once you sign the papers, the baby belongs to another family."

Rose responded quietly, "Yes, yes. Of course. Isn't this what you've wanted me to say all along? Just give me your papers and let me be on my way."

Kathryn had seen this type of behavior before and knew that she had to strike while the iron was hot. These girls finally realized the truth – that they were not fit to be parents. Rose's behavior demonstrated some degree of depression and in that state, she was more open to completing the necessary steps. Kathryn quickly withdrew all the appropriate forms from a desk drawer, put Xs every place Rose had to sign and shoved them across the desk at Rose.

"You won't regret this Rose," Kathryn said. "You're making a brave decision, one that will bring some lucky couple a great deal of joy." It was her usual closure, well-rehearsed after having said it so many times.

Rose never looked up. She felt disembodied, as if she were watching herself in a play. "Shut up," was all she said, scribbling her name in all the required places.

Ungrateful brat, Kathryn Baker thought. After all we've done for her around here.

When Rose got done signing away the life that was inside her, she proceeded to Mrs. Kellogg's office. The administrator and Dr.

Pickens were both there, waiting to see her. She walked in and sat down across from the big desk, focusing her attention on the pictures of babies behind Mrs. Kellogg. She thought back to her first visit to this office. She had never dreamed she'd still be here at this point.

"Rose, Dr. Oppenheimer tells us he's concerned about your mental state right now," Dr. Pickens began. "You've not appeared to have any particular issues other than what we've talked about related to your promiscuity. Can you tell me what is bothering you now?"

Rose looked at the psychologist and Mrs. Kellogg. She had no desire to tell them anything about how she was feeling.

"I'm quite fine, thank you. I just signed the adoption papers for Kathryn." Her voice was controlled and even. Her face was placid.

Mrs. Kellogg and Dr. Pickens looked at each other quizzically. "Dr. Oppenheimer was very certain that you may need some additional...help," Mrs. Kellogg said.

"Dr. Oppenheimer is kind to be so concerned," Rose said, "but I assure you I'm very well, indeed. Do you need me for anything else?"

Mrs. Kellogg looked at Dr. Pickens, who shrugged his shoulders – he had nothing else to offer.

"Very well, then, Rose. Please make sure you're taking care of yourself and following all the instruction that Dr. Oppenheimer has for you." With that, Mrs. Kellogg offered a dismissal.

Rose walked to the door. When she had placed her hand on the doorknob, she turned and said, "What happened to the parents who were supposed to receive Elizabeth's baby?"

"Oh, that was not a problem at all," Mrs. Kellogg said a little too cheerfully. "We gave them one of Deeny's twins. Isn't it a blessing that Deeny had twins? We were all so fortunate."

"Oh, indeed. We were all fortunate. Yes, everyone was very fortunate. Except for Elizabeth Eberly. She was not quite so fortunate, was she?" Rose said, and the sudden sarcasm in her voice struck the two administrators like a slap in the face.

Closing the door behind her, she realized that seeing the shock on Mrs. Kellogg and Dr. Pickens' faces was the first little bit of joy she had felt in a long time.

19

In the early evening of November 10, Rose started having more frequent Braxton-Hicks contractions, or so she thought. She had not been assigned any chores again that day, and she was grateful because she had been able to get some rest. The contractions were hard and uncomfortable. She remembered what Angie had told her...if the contractions start to come regularly, they're not Braxton-Hicks. She decided to read the materials the two nurses had given her one more time, measure the time between contractions, and get herself mentally ready for the hard work ahead.

She sat in her chair, and after a couple of hours, she realized the contractions were very consistent in their length, strength, and frequency. They were becoming generally more uncomfortable, and she considered lying on her bed. The papers said she did not need to go to the delivery room yet, and she wanted to stay in her own room as long as possible. She decided to get up and walk around for a bit and pray. She would lie down later.

She prayed as she paced, asking for God to help get her through the next few hours. She prayed for Liz and even talked to Liz. She prayed for and talked to Rafe, too. She had to believe their spirits were with her. It helped her feel less alone. The contractions were harder each time, it seemed, and a few times, the pain was so bad that she was forced to hold on to the bookshelf or sit down on her bed.

At about midnight, the contractions were very hard and only seven minutes apart. She thought she should go to the bathroom before walking upstairs to find the nurses. After she finished, she noticed some bleeding and some mucous coming from her. This must surely be it. The famous bloody show....

She left her room. The hall was as quiet as a church, and it was dark. Streetlights shining through the windows helped illuminate her way to the stairwell. Suddenly, a great gush of fluid came from her.

She gasped, mortified and frightened at the same time. She walked as quickly as she could manage up the steps to the third floor, heading straight to the nurses' sleeping rooms. She knocked on the door.

"Angie? Deb? Are you in there? I'm in labor." Frightened by what lay ahead, Rose sought the familiar – she needed to have her nurses with her now.

The door opened and a sleepy-looking older nurse said, "Hi. I'm June. Did you say you're in labor?"

"Yes, I'm certain of it. In fact, my water just broke. Is Deb or Angie here? Are you going to be helping me?" Her affect was flat, and the only emotion Rose showed was one of mild fear.

"I'm the only person here tonight," June tried to reassure this strange young woman, "but not to worry. When we have a delivery in the night, we call someone in. I'll get you settled, then make that call. I have to call the doctor, too."

June threw on her robe, took Rose to a labor room, and gave her a patient gown. "Put this on with the opening in the back – I guess you know that – and get into bed. I'll be right back, I promise." June smiled at Rose. "I know you haven't seen me – I usually work just in the delivery room. I have helped deliver many a child, and I promise, I'll help get you through this, ok? What time did all this start, anyway?"

Rose tried to speak, but a contraction hit her at that moment. "Oh, owww…this is hurting me," she moaned. "I don't know – maybe around 6 o'clock? The contractions were seven minutes apart when I started to come up here."

"Ok, good…I'll be right back." June disappeared, but reappeared in a very short time wearing surgical garb. "Dr. Oppenheimer is on the way, and both Deb and Angie will soon be here. I saw in your chart that they both wrote a note saying they wanted to be here when you deliver, so I called each of them. You'll have a good team, Rose. Now I need to check you to see how open your cervix is. Do you understand what I mean by that?"

"Yes, Angie told me about that," Rose replied. "Will all this take long?"

"Babies come when they're ready," June replied. The exam did not feel too great, but Rose tolerated it, closing her eyes.

"You're about seven centimeters dilated, and you're pretty well effaced – maybe 75% - and you're still at minus one station," June told her.

"What does that mean?" Rose inquired, another contraction starting up.

"Station is where the baby's head is located. You've got a little bit, Rose, but that's ok – you can do this, and besides, it gives us time for Angie, Deb, and the doctor to get here." June wrote information on Rose's chart.

"I feel like I've got to turn on my side," Rose said. "Is that all right?"

"Sure, Rose, whatever is most comfortable for you is perfectly all right," June replied to this sad, strange girl. She had not cared for Rose prior to this time and wasn't aware of all the events of her stay at Weingarten. Still, she felt sorry for Rose.

No more than twenty minutes passed when Angie and Deb both appeared in her doorway, smiling. They went to Rose's bedside and both hugged her.

"I'll go get the delivery room ready if you guys will take over here," June said, disappearing out the door.

"All right, now, Rose...here we go...baby time," Deb said.

"Are you all ready?" Angie asked.

"I guess so. I did try to eat a little more like you said, Angie, but I just haven't had a lot of appetite. I got some rest today, so that was good. And, oh - I finally signed the adoption papers." Rose looked at the shocked faces on either side of her bed. The nurses knew they should show support for the decision this mother had made, but they were surprised.

"Rose...are you sure about all that?" Deb asked her. "This decision has been such a struggle for you."

"I'm surprised, too, Rose. How did you come to that decision?" Angie spoke up.

Rose was expressionless and her eyes were focused on something distant. "Liz's death made me realize the baby will be better off with two good parents. What if something happened to me? The baby would have no one. My parents couldn't deal with it. I wouldn't *want* my brother. Rafe...who even knows where he is by this time? Kathryn and Dr. Pickens were right. This is my penance for being a 'bad girl' in the first place. Oh, wait...here's another contraction."

The two nurses looked at each other, worried. They didn't believe what Rose was saying. Deb shook her head and Angie knew what she meant. They had been too close, seen too much with this girl. They knew she was feigning acceptance.

"Rose, did Kathryn force you..." Angie started to say.

"No - don't...I don't want to talk about it anymore. The decision is made. The papers are signed," Rose said. "Oh God, here comes another one." She grimaced. "It feels like I'm being torn apart inside!"

"Maybe we better check you again," Deb said. "Angie, if you'll chart, I'll check." The two were an efficient team.

During the exam, another contraction came over Rose. They all realized the contractions were very close together now – no more than two minutes apart.

"You're dilated to nine, you're fully effaced. You're at plus two station. It won't be long," Deb said. She placed an oversized stethoscope on Rose's abdomen and listened. "The baby's heart beat is about 140 a minute, Ang...."

"Isn't that too fast?" Rose asked, eyes wide.

"That's perfectly fine...some people say if the baby's heartbeat is fast, it's a boy and if it's a little slower..." Deb never got to finish her statement.

"The baby's coming out!" Rose cried.

"Holy smokes...what the..." Deb lifted the covers from Rose, and the baby's head was starting to deliver.

"What the...? Angie, we can't even move her to delivery. Ok, Rose, get ready, this baby is coming out very soon. Take some deep breaths, ok?"

Angie pushed an intercom button in the room. "June, we're getting ready to deliver in here. Bring the delivery pack in here STAT!"

The nurses helped Rose get into position so that she could deliver the baby. "Keep taking deep breaths, Rose," Angie told her.

"Where's Dr. Oppenheimer?" Rose sounded frantic. "Oowww, this baby is coming out!"

"Don't push, if you can help it," Deb said. "Hang on, Rose. We're right here with you."

June rushed into the room, pulled up a small stand and put her delivery kit on top. She opened the package carefully, making sure she didn't touch anything inside with her bare hands.

"I have to push *right now!*" Rose yelled. "I can't stop it!"

"Angie, you're delivering this one," Deb said. "You or June...."

"Let me, June," Angie said, looking at her counterpart. "I've been with her so much."

"Gotcha. I'll chart." June took the clipboard and pen from Angie, who put on a surgery gown and a pair of sterile gloves. She got into position, sitting on the edge of the bed near Rose's feet.

"Rose, when you have a contraction, I want you to push. Do you understand? Bear down and push that baby out, ok?" Angie encouraged.

"Well it's coming right now!" Rose took a deep breath, bore down, and pushed as hard as she could to no avail.

"You're going to have to go again," Angie told her. "Next time...."

It was less than a minute before another contraction started. "Here it comes!" Rose exclaimed.

Once again, she took a deep breath and bore down without success.

"Rose, try pushing longer...it's hard, but you can do it. Concentrate, and next time, push longer," Deb said. "Remember, you can do it...it's all *you*, now."

"It's starting up again," Rose said. She took a very deep breath, focused on Angie at her feet and began pushing as hard and as long as she could while the contraction threatened to tear her apart. She felt something give, and at first, she feared that in fact, her uterus had torn apart. She would die like Liz. Then she heard a cry, loud and strong.

"Oh my God, Rose, you have a girl!" Angie shouted, and the other nurses started laughing.

Rose tried to catch her breath. That last push had taken everything she had. "Is she all right?" Rose asked between gasps.

"Oh yes, she's beautiful. Ten fingers. Ten toes. She's perfect!" Angie handed the baby to June, who wrapped her up in some kind of blanket. She was wiping the baby off and getting ready to put her in a bassinet. Deb was checking Rose's blood pressure, and Angie was preparing to deliver the placenta.

Hearing the baby's cry gave Rose energy. Now she wanted one thing and one thing only. "Can I hold her?" Rose asked, craning her neck for a glimpse of the child.

The three nurses stopped and looked at each other. "Rose, I still have to deliver the placenta, so give us a sec, ok?" Angie said.

"Oh, sure. I understand." Rose rested her head back against the pillow. She felt happy - happy that the delivery was over and that the baby was all right. She had almost forgotten what that felt like...happiness.

Dr. Oppenheimer appeared in the door, looking harried. "Don't tell me it's all over," he said. "I got here as fast as I could."

"Well, it was going along pretty routine and then all of a sudden, that baby decided it was time to come out," June told him as she continued caring for the newborn.

He walked over to look at the newborn. "Well, Rose, she's a beauty, that's for sure. How much does she weigh, June?"

"Eight pounds, eight ounces," June answered, "and she's twenty inches long."

"Perfect," he said. He pulled out his stethoscope and began examining the baby.

"Can I see her now?" Rose asked as she felt another little plop come out of her.

"The placenta is intact," Angie said.

"You guys! Can I see the baby? I'd like to see my baby." Rose's voice was insistent. The whole room grew quiet.

"Deb, how about a little Valium?" Dr. Oppenheimer quietly instructed.

Deb looked at the physician, shaking her head, disappointed in the same old approach to this issue. "How much?" she asked.

"Go ahead with 10 milligrams right now," he answered, crossing over to Rose. "Listen, Rose, holding the baby, even seeing the baby, is probably not in your best interest. We're going to give you some medicine to help with this part, because this will be sad for you. It is for just about every girl," the doctor told her as she began to well up. "Your baby is perfect and beautiful..." he paused. "And now she belongs to somebody else."

As Deb stuck a needle into her arm, Rose began to cry. "But why can't I at least see her? Even if I don't hold her, can't I at least see her? I've been carrying her around inside me all this time and I can't even see her?" She was distraught and becoming agitated.

"Add twenty-five of Phenergan to that, Deb," Dr. Oppenheimer said. "Rose, as your physician all this time, I have to make the decision that I think's going to be best for you. I'm sorry, but that's how it is. June, get that baby out of here."

June looked at him, then picked up the baby and left.

"No matter what, I should be able to see my baby!" Rose screamed. "Let me see my baby!" Then someone turned out the lights.

* * *

She awoke in her own room. Angie was sitting in a chair by the side of her bed dozing, her head beginning to nod. The clock said 6:30.

"Angie?" Rose said. The young nurse opened her eyes.

"Rose, I'm sorry. I must have nodded off there for a minute. It was a long night for you *and* for me." Angie smiled at her. "I'm going to check your fundus. You remember me telling you we'd be doing that, right? I have to make sure you're not going to have any bleeding."

"Where's the baby, Angie? I want to see her. I'm not going to keep her, but I want to see her." Rose was calm, but insistent.

Angie ignored the plea. "I'm going to push on your lower abdomen a little, hold on," she said. She looked to see if Rose was bleeding. "All is going well with you, Rose. The baby is doing good, too. She's beautiful."

"Angie, you and Deb have been as kind to me as any two people could be, but I'm begging you to please let me see my daughter."

"Rose, listen to how you're talking about this child! This is exactly why I wondered about you signing those adoption papers. You know that once you sign them, the baby is no longer yours. You're just a vessel to carry that baby to its destination. This baby is *not* your daughter." Angie sighed and sat back down in the chair. "If I show you that baby, I'm risking my job."

Rose remained quiet for a minute. "Just tell me where she is. Is she up on the third floor somewhere?"

"Yes, we have a small nursery with bassinettes. The baby is there," Angie told her.

"Then you don't have to show me. I'll find her myself. That takes you out of the middle," Rose answered. "I'll have another baby someday, but I'd like to see *this* baby before I leave this place."

"It won't work, Rose. Jenny is working in there today and she'll never let you in," Angie told her.

The two women sat quietly for a minute. Angie looked at Rose's face, remembering the sad girl she had been prior to the delivery. "I'd like to help you, Rose, but it's just all too late." She stood to leave. "I hope you can forgive me."

"Absolutely," Rose said. She had become more mechanical again. "Am I allowed to take a shower?"

"Yes, that's no problem. How do you feel standing up?" Angie asked. "Any dizziness?"

Rose stood up and took a few steps. "I'm completely fine. Thank you."

Angie watched as Rose went into the bathroom and closed the door. *This one is headed for problems*, she thought. *This is not going to end well.*

When she was done with her shower, Rose put on her robe and walked out of her room to the steps, beginning an ascent to the third floor. She had skipped breakfast and figured no one would miss her – they all surely knew by now that she had delivered. She felt unexpectedly strong and determined. She was finally going to see the product of the love she and Rafe had once had for each other. She tried to be as stealthy as possible. She thought everyone would still be in the dining room, but no use arousing any late sleepers.

At the top of the stairs, she turned right, heading toward Labor and Delivery. Her heart was beating so fast she thought it was going to come up out her throat. Her mouth was dry as she went through the Labor and Delivery door and looked to her right. 'Authorized Personnel Only.' Today, that's me, she thought. I'm authorizing myself to look in here.

She knocked lightly on the door, but she didn't know why she did that…what if Jenny's voice came from within? Would that stop her? Then she heard that voice. "Come on in."

Rose opened the door and quickly slipped inside. Jenny, her back mostly to the door, was holding a baby – the only one in the room – it had to be Rose's daughter. The nurse and baby were turned in such a way that she could see a little round, pink face revealed from the folds of the receiving blanket she was wrapped in. Rose could see dark hair – like Rafe. As Rose quietly approached, the baby blinked twice, then opened her eyes. They were blue-gray, but Rose could see the baby's eyes were going to be Rafe's too. She began to cry for the love she was handing over to complete strangers.

"Can I hold her?" Rose asked.

"Oh my God, what are you doing in here?" Jenny spun around to see that the person coming into this private space was not anyone she would have expected. "You must leave, immediately!"

Right at that moment, the door to the nursery opened. On a mission to check the readiness of the baby for new parents, Mrs. Kellogg and Kathryn Baker strode into the room.

"What is the meaning of this? Jenny, you surely know better than this!" Mrs. Kellogg was nearly shouting. Kathryn stood off to the side, shocked at the scene in front of her.

"I came in by myself, Mrs. Kellogg. It's not Jenny's fault. I just wanted to find my baby, to see her for one minute." Rose didn't want to give away that Angie had given her any information...Angie had been one of her only friends here.

"You had to have gotten the information about this room from someone," Mrs. Kellogg continued.

"No, I just came up and looked around," Rose said.

"That seems a little too convenient. Rest assured, I'll be getting to the bottom of this later. Rose, you will go back to your room now. This baby is not yours and it hasn't been since you signed the adoption papers." Mrs. Kellogg gave her an icy stare. "You'll be ready to go home very soon. In fact, I'll be calling your father today."

Rose suddenly felt desperate to know something about the adoptive parents. She reached for Kathryn's hands, trying to connect with some compassionate side Kathryn may have buried. "Please...who are they? The new parents, I mean. Are they kind? Will I meet them? Are they going to love my baby?"

Rose had hoped for compassion from someone who had none. Kathryn looked at Rose as if she were an imbecile and answered harshly. "Well, of course they'll love the baby. Would we entrust just anyone with these precious children? You know very well that we carefully vet the adoptive parents. We've discussed it many times, not that you ever paid much attention. And no, you will not be meeting them. The baby will be gone before you have your suitcase packed. Jenny, is the child ready to go?"

Jenny had backed away from the other women, holding the baby protectively. "Dr. Oppenheimer is satisfied that the baby is in good health. We'll give the parents the usual instructions." She could no longer look at the two women who had swooped in like vultures to take the newest hatchling out of the nest. She put the baby in a bassinette.

"Later today, I'd like to see you in my office, Jenny," Mrs. Kellogg told her. "I'm extremely disappointed in this occurrence and even though you may not be at fault, we will need to complete an investigation. We'll be back for the baby this afternoon if all goes as planned," Mrs. Kellogg said. "Please see to it that she is ready."

Rose began to cry. She started toward the bassinette, but Mrs. Kellogg reached out, grabbing her arm to stop her. "Take your hands off me!" Rose hissed, and something in her face made Mrs. Kellogg back away. Rose continued to the bassinette, looked down at the baby squirming in her blanket and said, "Some babies don't even get two parents who love them, but you'll always have four, little one."

She turned away from the little dark-haired newborn and approached Kathryn Baker. "Can you at least give the new parents this?" She reached into her robe pocket and pulled out a book – The House at Pooh Corner. Not knowing what to say, Kathryn took the book from Rose and looked away, remembering for the first time in a long time what embarrassment felt like.

Rose turned and walked quietly from the room. She had accomplished what she had come here for.

20

By the first of November, Rafe had not heard back from Henry Parker. He was anxious to know something – anything – in terms of what he might be able to do about Rose and the baby. On a Friday afternoon in November, he finally got a call from the attorney's office. It was the receptionist, Sally, asking if Rafe could come in the following Tuesday.

On November 12, Rafe was up early. He read the Tribune, looking for his story about the prior day's Veterans Day celebrations. He drank several cups of coffee, dumping out his last when he realized the caffeine was making him more edgy. He made sure to place his reporter's notebook in his jacket pocket, along with two pens, just in case one ran out of ink. He wanted to take copious notes to refer back to in case the memory of his conversation with Henry Parker failed him.

The walk up North Michigan was cloudy, cold, and windy, though not the worst he had experienced in Chicago. On days like this, he really longed for North Carolina – the warmth of the sun, the color of azaleas, and lazy afternoon drives. He picked up his pace and arrived at Steinbaugh, Deters and Parker a few minutes early.

"Good morning, Mr. Whitfield," Sally greeted him. "Mr. Parker will be just a minute. Can I get you some coffee?"

"No thanks," Rafe answered. "I've had my daily limit, plus some."

Sally just smiled and went back to her typing. Rafe sat down in one of the comfortable leather chairs in the waiting area and drummed his fingers on the arm in anticipation. He didn't realize how annoying he was till he looked up and saw Sally staring at him. She quickly looked back down at her work, and Rafe stopped his fidgeting.

The door to Henry's office opened, and he called to Rafe. "Come on in. Sorry to keep you waiting. I wanted to make one more phone call before I talked to you."

Rafe followed Henry to a conference table by the windows in his office. "Let's sit over here for this because I want to show you some of the things I've been looking at in regard to your case."

The comforting hand on Rafe's shoulder told him Henry was not getting ready to deliver good news. He felt weak all over and was glad to sit down. He tried to clear his head and focus on what Henry was getting ready to say.

"Rafe," Henry began, "looking back over as much history as I can find about the topic, and talking to anyone I know who has any expertise at all, unmarried fathers simply have few rights when it comes to their children. There have been some challenges to this, but they've largely been unsuccessful. I found a case where one man tried to challenge an adoption based on his Fourteenth Amendment rights to due process. His lawsuit failed. Even when the father can establish a biological link to the child, it's been difficult to try these cases and achieve any level of success. I know this is not what you want to hear, but it's the reality we're faced with right now. Do you know a standardized definition of 'father' doesn't even exist? Right now, the term for you would be a 'putative father'."

"What does that mean?" Rafe asked.

"It means that the legal relationship between you and the baby hasn't been established, even though you say you are the biological father. You're not married – you claim to be the father – but there's no way of really establishing a *legal* relationship," Henry explained.

"Good God, even when I am freely acknowledging paternity?" Rafe was incredulous.

"Sorry to say it, but yes. Rafe, there are a couple of other things you need to understand. In your situation, you are presumed to be 'unfit.' Before that comment makes you mad, let me explain…based on what I've found, Rose would also be considered 'unfit' to mother the child. That's how society looks at this, and our laws about your very circumstances reflect our current societal norms. So trust me, Rose is probably undergoing some brainwashing about her inability to mother a child, being told she's promiscuous and therefore the baby should go to a loving married couple…that kind of thing. What's more, she's probably hearing that nonsense on a nearly daily basis. Unfortunately, there's a whole crazy school of thought about this subject, and these so-called researchers tie the unsuitability of the mother and the father together. Let me show you something."

He pulled out a book by a woman researcher who was supposed to be an expert on the subject of unmarried parents. Henry opened the tome to a page he had bookmarked and pointed to a passage he had underlined. In the text, the author had called unmarried fathers, 'very often as neurotic as the mother.' Rafe slumped back in his chair and looked at Henry, whose face was sympathetic, compassionate and telling – there wasn't much hope.

"Now what?" Rafe asked.

"That depends on you, Rafe. I can pursue this. We can try to find Rose, and that will likely require a private investigator. They are not cheap – not the good ones, anyway. Then we'll have to prepare a case to be tried in North Carolina, or if Rose is in another state, we'd have to prepare according to the laws of whatever state she's been sequestered in. The bottom line is that this is going to be expensive and a long, drawn-out affair. You have to decide how much you can take, not only from an expense standpoint, but emotionally. You see, there's just no guarantee that if you do all these things, you'll be able to block an adoption. In fact, I can just about guarantee you that you *won't* be able to block the adoption. On top of that, by the time we'd be ready to go forward, there's a very good chance the adoption will already have been completed." Henry stopped. He felt drained. "This is terrible news for you, Rafe. I realize that. You don't think there's any reasoning with Rose's father?"

Rafe looked out the window. Chicago looked grayer and colder than when he had come to the office. In fact, it looked like it could snow. He thought about Hamilton Caswell and what a formidable man he was. Could he have any influence with him now that it was closer to the time Rose would be having the baby?

"I doubt it. He's got no use for me. I may try, though, because the fact of the matter is that I can't afford to go through all this. Neither can my parents. I'm sure they would help me, but I can't ask them to do that, especially when the outcome we'd hoped for seems so unlikely. I've gone through just about all the money I had saved for college. I did get in a couple of classes at Northwestern while I've been here, but I haven't finished college, let alone shell out the kind of money I'd need for an endeavor like this. I don't even know how much I owe you right now...." He trailed off, looking back to Henry. "How much *do* I owe you, by the way?"

Henry chuckled. "Rafe, I'm not charging you for this. I can't bring myself to it. Besides, I learned a lot that I may need to know at some point. I think the laws around all this are going to get turned upside down in a few years. I'll now have a little research behind me, so reviewing your situation has just moved me to the front of the class. This world is changing – I'll be more ready for those changes because I studied up on this."

"You're being generous," Rafe offered. "I can't let you do all this for free. I'm not *completely* broke – I do have a job." He smiled a little. "What about your billable hours?"

"Well, I'll tell you what. I can square all that with the guys. We all do some pro bono work. They'll understand it. And in payment, maybe you and I can have a beer with Melissa one evening."

"Only if you're sure." Rafe rose and extended his hand to Henry. "I'll never forget your kindness, I can tell you that."

Henry stood to reciprocate. "I wish I'd had better news for you." He paused. "Rafe, do you think there's some kind of providence in this? Maybe this really isn't the time to be getting married, having a child…maybe it truly is the time you should get focused on college, get your footing in life. I'm not trying to overstep boundaries in saying this to you, so I hope you take no offense, but sometimes things happen for a reason we don't understand right away."

Rafe stood quietly for a moment. "You know, I've occasionally wondered if I was being punished for getting Rose pregnant. I've asked God that question many times – 'are you punishing me?' – but I don't really think that's the case. I don't think God works that way. I'm not sure what I'm going to do. For now, I guess I'll keep working and trying to figure it out. I may end up calling Caswell, see if he'd even talk to me or reconsider his position. I have to think…."

"Well, again, I'm sorry I don't have better news. Let me know when you're ready for that beer," Henry said, walking Rafe to the door.

The two men shook hands again, and Rafe left, stepping back out into the cold Chicago day. There was a lot to think about, but it would have to wait - he had to get on to work. He was making good job progress at the Tribune; he was writing a little more all the time and learning so much. It was the best part of his life right now…it kept him from thinking about Rose every waking minute of the day.

Starting down the street for the Trib, he shoved his hands deep into his jacket pockets, feeling the notebook and pens still there. He had never written down a word.

21

Rose became a recluse during the long week she waited for someone to pick her up from Weingarten. She hardly ever came out of her room, and if she did, she spoke to no one unless she had been spoken to. Even then, it was perfunctory. She went to the dining hall, but she did not eat. The other girls came to think of her as somewhat of a freak - thin, pale, with stringy hair and clothes that were way too big.

Dr. Oppenheimer continued to check in on her. She was newly post-partum and he was obligated to see that she was all right, but he was also concerned about her. No one else in authority was particularly interested in her. Dr. Oppenheimer talked to Dr. Pickens about Rose one more time, feeling it was dangerous to send her home without addressing her depression. But Rose's baby had been successfully adopted, and as far as the rest of the administrators were concerned, her case was closed. After a few days, even Dr. Oppenheimer was too busy to worry anymore. He still had a home full of pregnant girls who needed his attention. It was the life he had chosen and he couldn't let one sad case get him off track…in reality, they were all sad cases.

Angie and Deb checked on Rose daily. They tried everything they could think of to cheer her up, talking to her about her family and parties she would attend at home, about getting ready to attend North Carolina State – just anything they could dream up that might help her focus on the future. None of it had much effect. Sometimes Rose would smile a bit, talk briefly about her mother or Miss Stella, but that was it. She never talked about her father or her brother. She didn't even talk about Rafe.

On the day of her departure, both Deb and Angie came to see her. They brought her a gift.

"We want you to have this…it's nothing big, but we wanted you to have something to remember us by," Angie told her, and she held out a gift-wrapped package, tied with a bow.

Rose sat in the chair by her window and opened the gift. It was a beautiful folding picture frame, which held two small pictures. On one side, was a picture of Rose and Liz, taken on the day of the Labor Day picnic they had goaded Miss Sullivan into arranging. Liz was pretending to stick a whole piece of cherry pie in her mouth, and Rose had her head thrown back, laughing, bright sunshine lighting up the girls' hair. On the other side, was a picture of Angie and Deb standing in the nurse's station, their arms around each other's shoulders, smiling broadly at the camera. Rose looked at the picture for a long time. Her eyes welled up.

"This already seems like a long, long time ago," she said in a whisper.

A sympathetic look crossed Deb's face. "Maybe that's better, really," she said.

The two nurses hugged Rose hard, said their good-byes and left just as Mrs. Kellogg came to get her.

"Your driver is here," she said. "Do you need any help with your belongings?"

"I'm not taking anything but my clothes. Everything else can stay for the next girl. I don't want any of it," Rose muttered.

"Very generous of you. Come along then, please." She bustled out and Rose gave the room one more quick look around. She picked up her suitcase, her volume of Wuthering Heights, and followed Mrs. Kellogg to the staircase. At the bottom, only Mr. Jenkins waited. *My own father couldn't drive me here, and he couldn't bother to pick me up,* Rose thought.

"Here she is. All the paperwork is signed and this packet should be delivered only to Mr. Caswell," Mrs. Kellogg stated to the driver.

"Thank you, ma'am," he answered. "Rose, are you ready? Do you have any good-byes left to say?"

Rose looked blankly at him for a minute. Then she turned to face Mrs. Kellogg. She took a breath and in a dead calm voice said, "I hope you always remember Elizabeth Eberly. I hope that every night when you lay down to go to sleep, you see her face in front of you." She turned back to a confused-looking Mr. Jenkins. "I'm ready now."

Mr. Jenkins picked up her suitcase, and they started the long journey for Kinston.

22

Rose's return to home was not much of an event. Upon her arrival, her mother fawned all over her, which only annoyed Rose. Daisy soon stopped trying, sensing that her overly demonstrative behavior was not welcomed. Stuart still seemed to spend a lot of his time out with his drinking buddies, which made Rose oddly jealous. And her father…he simply ignored her. She was an outsider in her own family. In a way, that was better. Rose wanted little to do with any of them.

Her only true champion was Miss Stella. She had always seemed more of a nanny to Rose than a servant, and Rose loved her. Miss Stella was the only person who could get Rose to do much of anything. She helped Rose get cleaned up and dressed in the mornings and made sure she had something to eat, even if she had to bring it to Rose's room. She brushed Rose's hair and curled it for her.

"Miss Rose, you cain't get feelin' no better if'n you don't take care of yourself," she would encourage Rose. But she could elicit little emotion from Rose. It broke the old maid's heart.

Rose was up at all times of the night. She slept in fits and starts, often dreaming of Liz or her baby. She didn't really think much about her life before pregnancy, including Rafe.

One night, when Rose was up wandering through the house, Stuart came home semi-sober. He found Rose sitting in her nightgown at the bottom of the stairs leading up to the second floor.

"Rose, what in the world are you doing down here at this time of the night? Waiting for me?" Stuart laughed. "I haven't had anyone waiting up for me for a long time, baby sister."

Rose looked at him, her face blank. Stuart wondered for a minute if she even recognized him. He sat down beside her.

"Rose, Rose…what has happened to you? Where is the girl who used to be the only light in this miserable house? Wake up in there, Rose, and come out."

Rose just stared at him. "Stuart, do you believe in Heaven?" she asked.

"What? What are you talking about, girl?"

"I want to know if you believe in Heaven. Do you?" Rose asked again.

Stuart scratched his head. "Rose, I don't think about it. I've never been the religious type. You know that. Oh, yeah, we had to go to church and so forth when we were little, but I never did see the point. So I guess the answer is no. I don't think I do believe in Heaven because I don't think I believe in God. There isn't some magic man up in the sky who fixes things. We have to fix them ourselves, I reckon."

"Then how do I fix my life?" Rose asked. "If God can't help me, how do I fix *me*?"

Stuart felt so sorry for his little sister at that moment that he could have cried. He had always had a tender spot for Rose. To see her this way was almost too much, even for someone like him whose heart had turned stone cold a long time ago.

"Rose, I don't know any answers. Think about it. We're all killing ourselves slowly. Daddy drinks too much, I drink too much, and Mama has taken so much abuse from Daddy that she's just about dead inside right now. There's a shadow on this family...it's been hanging over us since we were children. I don't know how to fix myself, let alone fix you. That shadow has kept us all from seeing any light. Don't you see it? That shadow has been around us all our lives." He stopped for a minute. "Rose, if there's anyone who can come out of that shadow, it's you. Give yourself some time."

Rose thought about his words. They were all killing themselves slowly. "I don't know how to pull out of it. I feel like I'm in a deep, deep hole – so deep and so dark I may never find my way out," was all she said. She stood and started up the steps, Stuart looking after her. He was filled with a sadness he hadn't anticipated.

"Little Rose, remember your big brother loves you," he said to the retreating form. "I always have. No matter what else, you're still my baby sister, and I love you very much."

She didn't respond with words, but looked back at him for a second or two and smiled the littlest smile before turning back to finish climbing the staircase.

* * *

The very next day at breakfast, Stuart talked to his parents about

Rose. Never one to confess anxiety, his worry about her mental state was genuine.

"Mama - Daddy," he began, "she's just about gone over the edge. Don't you think we should be doing something about it?"

"What exactly do you think we should be doing?" Ham replied. "She had good doctors in that home. If anything was wrong, they would have taken care of it there. She's just pining for that boyfriend of hers and probably pining for that baby, too."

"Daddy, I think it's more than that," Stuart said. "I don't usually fret too much over other peoples' problems, but I think Rose is doing more than just 'pining' for Whitfield or 'pining' for a baby. She's got something serious going on."

"What in blazes do you think you would know about it?" his father asked. "You can't get your face out of a whiskey glass long enough to learn anything about the world or know a thing about the people in it. When you get your own house in order, then you can tell me something about your sister's house. She'll be fine. She just has to let some time pass."

"Ham, if Stuart is concerned about Rose, maybe we should be, too. What if there's more going on, like Stu said? What if she's gone mentally ill?" Daisy spoke up.

"Woman, if she's 'gone mentally ill,' it would be because of some weakness in your lineage, I'm sure. Full of lunatics...that said, I do not believe she's mentally ill. She just needs time. She'll snap out of it." Ham put down his coffee cup. "There's not a problem in the world that can't be fixed by the passage of time. She'll come around."

"Daddy," Stuart began as he stood to leave, "I surely hope you're right about this one. You can say a lot of things about me and most of what you'd say would be true, but one thing you can never say is that I don't love my little sister...I do and I always have. It's not right, what you did to her, and it's not right what's happening to her right now, haunting this place like an old ghost. Mark my words. She is not doing well, and we're going to live to regret not doing something about it." He strode out of the room, leaving Daisy with her mouth hanging open and Ham snorting his derision.

* * *

Stuart went through that day at work angry – angry at his father, angry at his mother, angry at himself. He had never had enough courage to really stand up to his father. Ham controlled everything, including Stuart's very livelihood. The only thing Ham *hadn't* been able to control was Stu's party life, and that was the only way Stuart had been able to get through the days with his father. Deal with him all day; forget about it all at night, drinking with his buddies, an odd assortment of girlfriends, or strangers…it never mattered much to Stuart.

After work, he got in his car and drove aimlessly through town. He didn't even feel like seeing anyone he knew this evening. He drove by all the usual haunts, but there wasn't a place in town that appealed to him. He wanted to be alone with his thoughts and his frequent collaborator, Jack Daniels.

He left Kinston and drove until he saw a fork off to the left, leading down a dusty, unpaved road. He decided to take it, to see what might be down there. *The road less traveled. I'll have myself a little adventure*, he thought.

The road was uneven, bumpy. He got bounced around so much his kidneys hurt. He wondered about what shape his car would be in when he got back home that night. Then he saw a building in the near distance. It looked like a shack, almost, and when he got closer, he saw a smallish sign: The Topsy Turvy. There were a few beat-up old cars parked in the grass alongside the building. He decided to stop in. His red Corvette was a sharp contrast to the rusted-out trucks and other vehicles sitting there.

Stuart was surprised by the number of people inside the Topsy Turvy. The place was dark, but people sat around tables, each one dimly lit by a candle. Probably a fire trap, Stu thought. He couldn't make out any faces, but he could make out the bar, and he made a direct line for that. He perched on a barstool, looking around for any potentially familiar faces. Seeing none, he turned back to the ornate, mirrored bar, a sharp contrast to the rest of this shadowy, dirty dive.

"Bartender, I'll have a Jack and water," he called out to a sweaty, grisly-looking man behind the bar.

"No tabs," the bartender barked.

"I've got cash, you old chicken gizzard," Stuart snarled.

The bartender appeared with two glasses – one containing a tea-colored liquid and one half-full of water. "I'll let you mix 'em as you see fit," he said as he pushed the glasses towards Stuart.

"How much?" Stu asked.

"Dollar even," the bartender replied. As Stuart pulled out his wallet, the bartender looked at him closely. "Don't know that I ever seen you in here."

"You haven't...but depending on how fast you can keep these coming, you might see me in here again," Stu replied. He picked up the glass of Jack Daniels and downed it in a gulp. Then he took a sip of water. "May as well fill this back up while you're right here," he said, pushing the whiskey glass towards the bartender.

"That'll be another buck," the bartender answered, obliging Stu's request.

Stu drank, sipping his second whiskey a little more slowly. He was feeling the familiar burn in his stomach, enjoying the quick buzz that first shot had given him. He started thinking about Rose. Maybe a whiskey would serve her well. Maybe he'd ask if she wanted to come out with him sometime. He wouldn't bring her anyplace like this, though. He'd take her to some classy place in Goldsboro, or maybe even Wilmington...get her out of town....

The thoughts of a man imbibing by himself generally get a little more muddled with each drink. By the time he had finished off his eighth shot, Stuart was feeling no pain and wasn't really thinking about much of anything anymore. That was whiskey's purpose, wasn't it? To turn off your brain? He got out his wallet, put a ten-spot on the bar and slurred, "Hey, bartender. Just bring me the bottle."

"Boy, you have had just about enough. I don't believe you need a bottle right now. What you need is a cup of coffee, which I do not have here. Just drink your water for now." The old bartender had seen just about one too many puking drunks in his life and he didn't feel up to it tonight.

"C'mon, old timer. At least give me one more," Stuart said.

"One more, and that's it," the bartender gave in. "Boy, what's your name, anyway?" he asked as he poured Stuart's drink.

"Stu Caswell," he answered.

"Ham Caswell's boy?" the bartender asked.

"Yup. The one and only," Stu turned away to face out towards the rest of the bar, not noticing that a man sitting next to him had raised his head to look at Stuart upon hearing the Caswell name. The man stood up and walked over to a table, leaned down and whispered something to the men sitting there, who rose in unison and walked over to face Stuart.

"You Stuart Caswell?" one of the men asked.

"Yeah. What's it to you?" Stu replied, too drunk to recognize the ominous looks on the faces of these strangers.

"You work for your old man, Ham Caswell?" another man asked.

"Yeah, I do. So what?" Stuart said, quickly impatient with the questions.

"You know Wesley Ammons?" the first man asked, narrowing his eyes.

"That thief? Yeah, I know him. In fact, I had the pleasure of firing his ass." Stuart laughed and hiccuped. "He was a no-account if I ever saw one. If you gentlemen will excuse me, I gotta go take a leak. Bartender, can you point me to the men's room?"

"The 'men's room' is outside – out back," the bartender growled. "Help yourself."

Stuart went to the outhouse, disgusting as it was, and relieved himself. He realized he was drunker than he should be and went straight to his car. Waiting by his car were the men who had been talking to him inside the bar.

"What can I do for you boys?" he asked as he approached. "Admiring the ride?"

The man who had first spoken to him stood between Stuart and the Corvette. "Oh yeah, I'm admiring the ride all right. Must be nice to have money for a car like this one right here, and your daddy's got all the money in the world, don't he?"

Something in the man's tone made Stu uncomfortable. The group of men seemed menacing now, out here where there was no longer any light but that of the moon.

"Well, he's pretty loaded, that's for sure, and so am I, so if you gentlemen will excuse me, I'm going to head for home and sleep this off," Stuart tried to mollify. He started around the man toward his car, but the man grabbed his arm.

"You don't know me, do you?" he asked Stuart, who tried to mask genuine alarm. His drunken haze kept him from thinking clearly, kept him from knowing how to handle this confrontation.

"No sir, I don't believe I do. Who are you?" he asked, trying on a smile that was more of a grimace.

"I'm Waylon Ammons, Wesley's brother. You know he ain't been right since you beat him half to death last spring? My mama has to feed him and wipe his behind for him. Whatcha say about that?"

Stuart had no words. He tried to think of something to say, but nothing would come. He was petrified; for the first time in his life, he was truly scared.

"I…I…" he stammered.

Waylon Ammons punched him hard in the gut. Stuart doubled over. "Wait, wait…" he choked out. "I didn't know. I had no idea." It was hard to make the words come out. Waylon had just about punched the air out of him.

"Of course you didn't know, you rich bastard. And you never cared to find out, did you?" Waylon spit out. "Well now you're going to get some of your own medicine." The group of men moved closer to Stuart.

"Wait, now. I didn't know. Use this to take care of him." He pulled out his wallet and handed Waylon Ammons a wad of bills. Stuart didn't even know how much he handed him.

Waylon took the money, looked at it for a moment, then threw it on the ground in disgust. "You think *money* can make up for what you did to my brother? You think your *money* can make up for my mama's broken heart?" He grabbed Stuart by his shirt, pulling his face in close. "He didn't deserve what you done to him, and now you're gonna pay all right, but not in dollar bills," and he punched Stuart again.

This time, Stuart hit the ground. He writhed around, trying to catch his breath, but he was in serious pain. One of the men pulled him up to his feet by the back of his collar, and Waylon hit him again, this time in the face. His jaw was broken by the power of Waylon's punch, and he spit out some blood and teeth. He knew these boys weren't done with him.

Once again, Stu was jerked to his feet. Just as Waylon reared back to take another swing, Stuart twisted away from the man who had pulled him up and ran for the Corvette. The men were giving chase, pulling at him, but he was able to slip out of their grasp. He was lucky that he had left his car door unlocked; lucky that the men had all been drinking, too, and were just as clumsy as he. He got in the car and quickly locked the door. He heard the men yelling, but he couldn't make out the words and didn't want to. He fumbled in his pocket for his keys as the men began pounding on the windows and roof of his car. The key in the ignition, Stuart turned it and put the car in gear as fast as he could coordinate the efforts. He backed up, nearly running over one of the men, then pulled out of the grassy parking lot, leaving a wake of torn up grass and dirt. The men chased him out to the road, and in his rearview mirror, he could see them pile into one of the pickup trucks and begin following him. He pushed the accelerator and smiled to himself. It hurt like hell to smile, but he couldn't help himself; they'd never catch him now.

He kept the accelerator pushed almost to the floor, shifting gears as the Corvette roared along the unfamiliar dirt road. He was going so fast, and the road was so bumpy that he was nearly airborne more than once, but he knew he couldn't let up. Those boys meant to kill him.

Those boys didn't have to. All they had to do was chase a drunken Stuart Caswell, letting him find out how hard it is for a drunk to speed on an unfamiliar highway. Some distance behind, Waylon Ammons and his cousins heard a loud crash and saw a low orange glow between the Carolina pines, which soon became a bright yellow inferno. They stopped and watched in silence for a minute, unable to hear the screams emanating from the Corvette. They turned the truck around and headed back for the Topsy Turvy.

23

"Hello?" Rafe answered the phone on its fifth ring. He hadn't been home from work for five minutes, having stopped for drinks with Melissa and Henry Parker. He had walked all the way to his apartment from The Goat in the cold December wind. Rafe decided 'The Windy City' was the right nickname for Chicago.

"Rafe, it's Dad. I'm glad I caught you. Have you got a minute?" Glenn Whitfield didn't sound exactly like his normal, cheerful self, filling Rafe with dread.

"Sure Dad...what's up?"

"Stuart Caswell is dead." Glenn said no more, waiting.

"What? How?" Rafe was stunned. Stu had always seemed like one of those guys who would live hard forever - a cat with nine lives.

"Car accident – a bad one. We've been told they think he was burned alive," Glenn told him, somber as a priest.

"Good grief, that's horrible! When did this happen?" Rafe was truly in shock. He had never been close to Stuart, but he knew what kind of pressure Ham had put on him all his life. Succeed! Take no prisoners! Win at all costs! Stuart had turned out to be nothing like Ham.

"Just two weeks ago," Glenn answered.

"God in heaven, Dad, why didn't you call me? Did Rose come home?" Rafe asked.

"Yes, son." Glenn paused for a second. "Rose is home. We saw her at the funeral."

Rafe went silent, his throat closing, choking him. At least that's how it felt. After a minute, he heard his father say, "Rafe?"

"I'm here, Dad. I'm just trying to take it all in. How did she look?"

"Bad, son, truth be told. She looked very bad," Glenn answered.

"How so? What do you mean by 'bad'?"

"She's pale. She's so thin she looks like a bag of bones. All the while her mother was sobbing at the funeral, Rose stared straight ahead. She showed no emotion at all…it was strange. It's like our old Rose isn't even inside that girl we saw. Your mother and I were shocked. We tried to talk to her, to offer our condolences, but she didn't even seem to recognize us. She looks like a girl who has lost her mind. I'm sure sorry to tell you this, son, but that's how she seemed."

Rafe could barely process the information his father was giving him. He sat down on a chair, telephone receiver still at his ear, and was quiet again.

Finally his father said, "Rafe, are you all right? Are you still there?"

"Yes Dad, I'm still here. I am just floored by all this. Did she have the baby with her?"

"No son, no baby…." Glenn left the words hanging in the air between Kinston and Chicago.

Rafe hung his head for a minute, then sat up straight.

"Dad, I'm coming home. I'll give notice at the Trib and come home as soon as I can. Maybe I can help Rose. One thing I know…she can't be alone in that house with Daisy and Ham. If she has any sanity left, it won't last long with only those two around."

"I'm happy to hear you say that, son. In fact, there's just one more thing," Glenn started.

"Good grief, Dad, haven't you told me enough bad news?" Rafe said.

"This isn't bad news…there is one small good thing to tell you about. Jim Fussell called. He's leaving the Free Press - retiring - and needs someone to take over. He asked about you."

"Dad, I don't know. I mean, I've had a couple of classes now, but to run the paper? Even a small one…I've gotten some on-the-job knowledge and experience. I don't know…."

"Don't need an answer on that right this second, son. You can consider all that on your way home. Just think about at least talking to Jim."

"All right, Dad – I will. You know I have to give a two week notice at work and at least a month on the apartment, unless they'll let me out of the lease. Housing is tight here in the city, so maybe…I'll work on it. Anyway, I'm glad you called." Rafe felt exhausted.

"I wish I was calling with all good news, but that's just not life is it?" Glenn said, sounding tired himself.

"Tell Mom I said hi and that I love her. I'll keep in touch with you about what's happening on my end and when I think I can get home, ok?" Rafe told him.

"All right son, just let us know. We both love you. Take care of yourself till we see you." The two men hung up, and without conscious purpose, Rafe began to pray for Rose.

* * *

At the Caswell mansion, a black wreath hung on the front door, but only Miss Stella wept in private for the grandson she had never been able to publicly confess. How could it be that her only child, Daisy, couldn't even cry for Stuart?

The old woman thought about the ragged road she had traveled for her life to get to this point. Maybe it was her burden to bear because she had gotten pregnant by a white boy at age fifteen. Just a child herself, she couldn't provide any kind of life for Daisy, whose skin had stayed amazingly pink. When Daisy became a beautiful young woman, they were still poor as dirt; Stella had pushed her at Hamilton Caswell for all the wrong reasons – Daisy could "pass." Stella realized a long time ago that she had made a mistake, but by that time, it was too late.

Daisy wouldn't leave her mother behind when she also got pregnant and subsequently married into wealth. Never wanting to cause embarrassment for the Caswell name, Stella had worked as a servant for her own daughter and son-in-law. But there was no amount of money that could make up for the beatings her Daisy had suffered while she watched in silence, and no amount of money could make up for the heartache she now felt. All that was left was Rose. She would make up for it all by taking care of her granddaughter, the girl who only knew her as a maid.

24

Days and weeks passed without Rose showing any improvement. She wandered around the house like a specter, rarely even going outside. Miss Stella finally convinced Rose to go for a walk with her one day, but it was an unusual occasion for the young woman to even come out of her room, let alone the house. She spent most of her days sitting by her window, staring outside or looking at the pictures Angie and Deb had given her when she left the Weingarten home. Sometimes she would look at pictures of herself and Stu when they were little, but she didn't register any emotion as far as anyone else in the house could ascertain.

Miss Stella continued to care for her, helping her with daily living activities such as bathing, washing her hair, and getting dressed. *This is a gone girl*, Stella thought, her heart breaking for her granddaughter. She cared for Rose with great tenderness and compassion, the way she wished she would have cared for her own young Daisy when she was in trouble.

Daisy would stop in every day and twitter at Rose about some ladies' activity she had been involved in. She thought maybe if she talked to Rose about her busy life, Rose might start to reconnect to the world. Daisy loved Rose but was incapable of mothering her now. Rose barely acknowledged her on these visits.

Ham looked in a few times, just sticking his head inside the door, almost as if to see if Rose was really there. He might offer a greeting, but not much else. A man of little insight, he had no ability to deal with someone who was as severely depressed as his only living child had become.

No one knew what Rose thought about in her solitude. Her face was blank all the time. She spoke rarely, and when she did, it was so quiet that no one could be sure of what she said. During Rose's bath once, Miss Stella thought she heard the girl whisper something about blood on the floor. Miss Stella looked all over Rose's room, but found nothing.

Christmas morning came and went. Daisy had made sure the house was decorated, gifts were purchased, the traditional multi-layered cakes were baked. She had attempted to make the environment as normal as possible in a home that was anything but normal. There were no grand Christmas parties this year. The circumstances of Stuart's death still loomed over them as a mystery. Rose was out of her mind, Stuart's death coming like the final blow to her already fractured psyche. Hamilton was not interested in any of the affairs of the house. Daisy was on her own.

The calendar finally said 1969. *A new year, a new start*, Daisy thought. *Maybe things will get better.*

And they did. Rose seemed to be unraveling her fugue. She was still a walking shell, gaunt and anemic-looking, but she started coming downstairs for at least one meal a day. Daisy was happily surprised to see Rose wearing a sweater she had gotten her for Christmas. Hamilton was satisfied that his prediction was correct...Rose just needed time. She still didn't speak much, but would offer a 'good morning' or a 'good evening' as appropriate. She walked outside a little more, not needing encouragement from Miss Stella, who thanked God that the girl she had loved from birth seemed to finally be coming around.

And then came a bright, sunny February morning; a beautiful day, really. Rose walked into the dining room with a yellow dress on. Daisy had seen her wear it before, but it had been a long time. Rose had lost so much weight that the dress hung loosely on her scrawny frame, but Rose had a smile on her face. Daisy recognized a necklace that the Whitfield boy had given Rose a year ago. It was a silver chain with a small square piece of glass. The glass pendant preserved a tiny four-leaf clover. "Oh, Rose, darling, you look wonderful this morning! I'm so happy to see you dressed up a little," Daisy exclaimed, rushing from her seat at the breakfast table to put her arm around Rose's shoulder. "But dear, it's a chilly day. Shouldn't you wear something a little warmer?"

"No, thank you." Rose was mechanical, but functioning. Daisy couldn't have been happier.

Ham looked up from the morning paper, somewhat surprised, but even more smug about Rose's progress than he had been before. If only the women would listen to him, they'd see he was usually correct about these things.

Rose took a place at the breakfast table. She drank a sip of orange juice, then sat quietly with her hands folded in her lap, looking like a waif and a princess at the same time.

"Daddy, may I borrow one of the cars this morning?" Rose asked.

Shocked, Ham put down the paper and looked sternly at Rose. "Do you think you're ready to drive? You haven't driven in a year, almost. Where are you going?"

"You make a good point, and that's why I'm asking. I haven't driven in a long time, so I just want to get some practice - get a feel for it again," Rose answered.

Both Ham and Daisy were surprised and confused by this sudden change in a girl who had still seemed so morose the very day before.

"How about if Mr. Jenkins comes with you, just to give you some reminders and so forth?" Daisy asked, hoping Rose would take her up on the suggestion.

"No, it makes me more nervous when people are giving me instructions. Remember when I learned to drive?" Rose said.

"All too well," Ham said. "Daughter, the answer is yes, you can have a car. Just name which one you want."

"It's just me. Can I take the Mustang?" Rose asked.

Hamilton was thrilled that she would ask for the Mustang. Her choice showed some level of energy he had not seen in Rose for a long time.

"Of course you can have the Mustang. Take it out and have some fun for a change." He went back to his newspaper, then said, "Daisy, make sure Jenkins knows to get it gassed up for her."

"Certainly," Daisy said, but some unidentifiable apprehension gripped her. She couldn't begin to understand what had caused such a swing in Rose's behavior…one day like a lost soul; the next, almost her old self.

Daisy went out into the hallway, where Miss Stella was watering a plant. "Miss Stella, Rose is going out in the car today."

Miss Stella almost dropped her watering can, sloshing water onto the hardwood floor. "By herself?" she asked as she stooped to wipe up the spill.

"Yes. Can you have Mr. Jenkins make sure the Mustang has a full tank? And then, can you let him know what is going on? Maybe he can follow her a little way and make sure she's all right."

"Yes ma'am, I will do 'xactly that." Miss Stella bustled off to find the driver.

Daisy went back into the dining room where Rose had finished her orange juice – she hadn't eaten a bite. "Rose, if you're going out, don't you think you should eat something? You'll need it for strength."

"I'm *fine*, Mother!" Rose snapped, then she recovered her poise. "I'm sorry. Don't worry. Maybe I'll stop somewhere and have lunch."

"Well, all right dear, but do wear a warm sweater or jacket, all right?" Daisy gave in.

Rose went to her room and conceded to her mother's advice...a jacket would do today. She looked at herself in the mirror. Hair combed, face scrubbed clean, nice shoes and her yellow dress. Today would be a good day.

Mr. Jenkins had the car ready for her, and she slowly pulled away from the house. She followed the circular drive around to the long, long lane she had roller skated on so many times as a kid. How she had loved those simple days. Back then, even her father had been softer, kinder, had treated her with great tenderness. She was his little Rosebud.

She moved onto the highway. It felt good to be behind the wheel, but a little unnerving, too. She thought of her brother, Stuart, and the horrible crash that had taken his life. It didn't matter to Rose that he was probably drunk. He didn't deserve the fate he had come to.

Rose looked in the rearview mirror...she thought the car behind her might be following her. Of course. Her father or mother would have asked Mr. Jenkins to keep an eye on her. She drove into Kinston and parked in front of a dress shop she used to frequent. She started to get out of the car, then saw that Mr. Jenkins passed on by. He would think she had decided to just go shopping. Rose waited for a few minutes to make sure he didn't return, then started the car again, heading for Goldsboro.

Goldsboro was about a thirty-minute drive. Plenty of time to think about what she wanted to do, plenty of time to revise her plans for the day if she wanted to. She drove without looking at the scenery she loved so much; the tall, long-needled pines; the red dirt that ran like a ribbon alongside the highway. She had always been proud of her home state; had always thought that North Carolina was a beautiful state, but it was lost on her as she focused on the road ahead.

By noon, she was in Goldsboro. A few things had changed since the last time she was here. It was almost a year ago since she last enjoyed Wilber's barbeque. She stopped in, ordering ribs and tea. It was the best meal she had eaten in a year. She took her time, savoring the flavors, spicy and sweet, wishing Liz could have been with her – *how she would have enjoyed this food!* - and thinking about the times she had come here with Rafe.

When she left the restaurant, she headed out for Seven Springs. It wasn't far from Goldsboro, but Rose pushed the accelerator a little, anxious to reach her destination.

She parked the car near the bluffs, wanting to survey the Neuse River from up high. It was a crisp, beautiful day for her walk, and as she made her way to the place where the river had carved a gorge through the limestone, she prayed aloud.

"God, where were you when Rafe and me told Mother and Daddy about the baby? Where were you when my daddy shipped me off to a hateful place with hateful people? Where were you when Lizzy died? Where were you while Stu burned to death? Have you been hiding from me?" She paused, looking up at the sky. "*Have you been hiding from me?*" she screamed, stopping at the edge of the gorge and looking down into the murky, muddy river. "You might have been hiding from me, but I haven't been hiding from you." Tears streamed down her face. "I haven't been hiding from you," she repeated. "Do you see me?" She lifted her head and looked at the sky. "I'm right here."

Rose reached up and took off the necklace Rafe had given her. She held the pendant in her hand and looked at the four-leaf clover, thinking about what it had represented to them. "For luck," Rafe had said when he gave it to her. Was there even a chance they could still have any good luck? She fumbled, dropping the necklace, and she couldn't see where it went. *Well, so much for good luck*, she thought. *Why would I expect to have any now?*

She had been here many times and knew the landscape well. A smile crossed her lips as she took in the view, a favorite. Then she extended her arms out to the sides and felt the cold February wind lift her up and off the craggy rock precipice.

Why, it's just like flying, she thought, happier than she had been in a long time.

*   *   *

What Daisy and Ham couldn't figure out that morning, Angie Sweeney and Deb White would have been able to tell them...that a person as depressed as Rose often has an unexplained surge of energy before making a crucial final decision to end their own life. Now only the Neuse River would understand; for two million years, the Neuse kept its secrets and left nothing behind...nothing except the broken bodies of the broken-hearted who soared from high cliffs to the rocky river bottom.

25

Rafe never could have dreamed that in the stretch it took him to get back home, he'd arrive just in time to help the community of Kinston begin a search for Rose Caswell. Organized by the Lenoir County sheriff, volunteers who had either been friends with the Caswell family or had worked for them came together for meetings about how to proceed – what territory to cover, what size groups would work together, what to do if they found her alive, what to do if they came across her body somewhere. He and his father volunteered to help with the search. Not knowing her state of mind, it was hard for Rafe to think about where she could be.

Day after day, Rafe joined the search. His father had to work, of course, but Rafe was still free. He hadn't had time to sit with Jim Fussell to talk about the Daily Free Press. There was plenty of time for that once Rose had been located.

He talked to Melissa in Chicago and told her what had transpired while he was on his way to Kinston. She was a sympathetic ear, even offering to take vacation to come help with the search. Rafe didn't think he wanted her there. He wore his fear and grief on his sleeve now, and he just didn't feel he could handle anyone sharing that with him.

He kept to himself, talking only to his parents and the occasional friend from high school who had stuck around town. Rose was all anybody talked about. What had happened? Was she kidnapped? Had she been murdered? Did she just go off on her own? Not knowing was horrible, but listening to the constant speculation was worse.

His mom would sometimes come with him to the volunteer headquarters. Anne never went on the searches, but she stayed by the phone or made coffee for the volunteers. With temperatures in the thirties, most everyone needed regular breaks to warm up. She brought supplies to make sandwiches. Daisy Caswell was often in the headquarters, too, but she was barely functional. Anne tried to keep her occupied, asking her to help get lunch ready for the volunteers.

The sheriff was as puzzled as anyone. This type of thing didn't happen in Lenoir County much. He talked at length with Mr. Jenkins after Ham told him that the old driver had followed Rose for them on the day she went missing. Mr. Jenkins faithfully reported what he knew; that the last time he had seen the young woman was in front of Lucille's Dress Shop, getting out of her Mustang. He felt certain she was going shopping, but no one in the dress shop remembered ever seeing Rose actually come in. She had simply disappeared, leaving no clues for anyone to follow.

Racking his brain while he walked to the volunteer headquarters one morning, Rafe thought about all the places Rose loved the best. He went over everything he could remember, mentally re-examining conversations they had about places she wanted to go. She might have decided to just clear out and go start life in a town she loved. Could she have gone to Wilmington? She loved the beach. What about Asheville? She had talked about how beautiful she thought that area was. But those places seemed like farther distances than Rose might go by herself. Then he thought about Goldsboro. She like to go there to eat or go to the park once in a while, just for something different to do. It was only about a half hour away. She had always loved the bluffs....

The bluffs. Rafe cringed and didn't want to think about what that could mean, but knew he had to mention it to the sheriff. He picked up his pace so that he would be there before the volunteer groups broke up to go out and search for the day.

Sheriff Logan was still in the headquarters when Rafe got there. Logan often did not go on the searches himself, but he usually helped get things organized each day. He looked up when Rafe entered the conference room where everyone met, and the boy was white as cotton. At first, the sheriff thought he might be sick, but the look on Rafe's face told him there was something more going on. He saw cold fear in Rafe's eyes. Everyone in town knew the boy had loved Rose. It was clear to Logan that Rafe knew something - maybe something that would help them locate the Caswell girl. Rafe proceeded directly to the front of the room and pulled the sheriff aside. Most of the volunteers were starting to move out.

"Sheriff, maybe everyone should wait for a minute..." he began. "I've had a thought. I could be wrong, and I hope I am...."

"Everyone...folks, please stick around for a minute – don't go quite yet." Logan and Rafe moved to a corner of the room while the others milled around, conversing quietly. "What is it, Rafe? Have you seen or heard something?"

"No sir. But I think I might know where she could have gone," Rafe said, having difficulty even saying the words. "Goldsboro. The bluffs at Seven Springs. Cliffs of the Neuse. She loved that place. We should look there."

The sheriff paused and considered this thought for a minute. "You seriously think she could have gone there? For what purpose?" Then his mouth opened slightly - he knew. "Do you want to come with me?" Logan asked. "I'll go myself today. You can ride along if you want. You've been here every day...."

"I don't know if I can," Rafe started. "Maybe I can ride along but just not walk out to the bluffs with you...."

"That's fine, son. Whatever you think is best," Logan told him. He put his hand on Rafe's shoulder. "Don't think I don't know how hard this has been for you, Rafe." That was all he said, and it was enough. Rafe began to shake violently. He had to sit down. By this time, all the volunteers were looking at the two men whose discussion had appeared so intense to them. The entire room of people starting inching their way towards the duo, curious about what had transpired between them.

"Folks, we think we might have an idea about where Rose Caswell could have gone. I'm going to ask only two of you to come with me and Rafe, here. We're going to ride over to the Goldsboro area," Logan announced. "Jimmy Wood and David Greeley – can you two come along with me today?"

The two men quickly moved forward, nodding their assent. The others started to scatter when a voice from the dispersing group spoke up, "Sheriff, you want us to continue to look around here?"

"Y'all have been helpful all these days, but why don't we suspend this for today, let us take this ride to Goldsboro and see what transpires from there. I'll radio the office and let them know what's going on," the sheriff replied. He turned to Rafe. "You sure you want to come along, son? You're mighty white-looking. You need some water?"

Rafe sat, head in hands. He knew he had to go along. He had to be there in case they found Rose.

"I'll be all right. I'm coming along. I want to call my folks first," he said.

Rafe's mother discouraged him from going along. "Rafe, are you sure? You could be in for a horrible discovery," Anne said tearfully. She was every bit as scared as Rafe to think about the unthinkable.

"Mom, I have to go. I just have to," he answered. His voice was full of despair, yet determination. Anne was aware she couldn't win this argument.

"All right, son. I'll pray."

Rafe knew she would be doing exactly that.

The trip to Goldsboro seemed to take forever. Logan was driving slowly, intentionally not going one bit faster than the speed limit. He had been a law enforcement officer for a long time, and he knew that when he was tense, he had to stay very focused, each action controlled, deliberate. Jimmy and David spoke quietly to each other in the back seat. Rafe, sensing that the three other individuals were as tense and worried as he was, kept his thoughts to himself.

They drove down the main drag in Goldsboro and didn't see Rose's car. That diamond blue Mustang would stick out like a sore thumb. They went down a few secondary streets, then left town, heading for Seven Springs.

"We should go right to the cliffs," Rafe said. "That's the only place she would be." Foreboding now filled his heart.

Twenty-five miles is a long ride when you dread the destination. The men were all quiet during the ride, only the occasional crackling dispatch over the sheriff's radio breaking the silence.

Once they reached Seven Springs, the sheriff went straight to Cliffs of the Neuse State Park. This was a happy place for thousands of people who hiked here every year. At the turn of the century, visitors had come to drink mineral water, thinking it would cure all kinds of maladies. They took riverboat rides to see those magnificent cliffs, rising ninety feet above the muddy water, painted like a rainbow of tan, yellow, brown and white. The Cliffs were a beautiful place to go when you wanted to see God's handiwork or to just enjoy some solitude. They had once been a happy place for Rose and Rafe, too.

His heart sank when they pulled into the park. Rafe saw the Caswell's Mustang in the first parking lot they came to. Sheriff Logan radioed a partner and told him what the men had found and told them that they'd be there a while. His deputy told Logan he'd call the police in Seven Springs and get some help out at the park. The four men began walking, Greeley and Wood ahead of the Sheriff and Rafe.

"If you find anything, holler. Don't touch or move anything," Logan instructed them.

"Don't worry about that! The last thing I want to touch is a dead body!" Greeley called back to him.

Logan looked at Rafe. "Ignore that, son. Chances are that we'll find her lost in these woods somewhere. According to her mama and daddy, she hasn't been in her right mind, really, but had perked up on the day she left in the car. Hold on right here for a minute. I don't want to go too far because I imagine the Seven Springs boys will be out here directly."

The two men waited at the trailhead and Rafe asked, "How long can someone go without food and water? She's been out here for days. Could she even be alive?"

"Well that depends at least partly on what kind of shape she was in when she got here. If she's strong, yes, she could get by. She'd have to find things to eat and have to get some water. The river isn't too clean anymore, but it wouldn't kill her," Logan answered.

They waited in silence after that. Logan was thinking of all the things he had waiting for him at the office, and Rafe was thinking about all the terrible things that could happen to Rose in this park. He was trying unsuccessfully to pray for her when the Seven Springs police drove up. Logan went to meet them. The officers all stood by their patrol car, occasionally looking at Rafe as Logan filled them in. They had heard about Rose's disappearance. That kind of thing didn't happen much in small towns, so when it did, it was big news. The men finally approached, and Rafe stood to accompany them on the trail.

"Son, I've asked you before, and I'll ask you again…are you sure you want to do this part?" Logan asked Rafe.

"I don't think so, to be honest, but I have to do something, and if she's alive, she knows me and may respond better to me than to any of you men. No offense intended," Rafe apologized.

"None taken," one of the Seven Springs officers said. "I'm Officer Downey, and this is my partner, Officer Martin. We have a couple of places in mind that we think we should start looking, if you gentlemen would like to follow along. Or, you can go down another trail if you think you have an idea of an area she would have been familiar with."

"I know a spot she loved. I think Sheriff Logan and I should go there and y'all could go where you think best," Rafe answered.

The parties went their separate ways after the officers coordinated radio frequencies for communication. It didn't take long for Rafe to lead the sheriff to the high cliff Rose had always liked to stand on. The view was spectacular, but yielded nothing. It didn't look like anyone had been on this spot for some time. They stood there for a while, warming in the sunshine, surveying the area for any sign, any clue. They had turned to leave when something caught the sheriff's trained eye. A brief glimmer – the sun had reflected off something shiny, out of place in the dense green underbrush. He carefully picked his way down a grassy part of the cliff adjacent to the rocky prominence. He tried to keep his eye on the area where the shiny thing had sparkled in the sun. When he had eased himself close enough, he reached down and pulled up a silver chain. Rafe watched as Logan made his way back up to the top of the cliff.

"Does this look familiar to you?" he asked Rafe as he came closer and held up a four-leaf clover pendant.

Rafe looked at the sheriff, his eyes welling up. His shoulders began to heave, and he sank down on the ground, the hot tears spilling over, blurring his vision. "It belongs to Rose. I bought it for her. It was supposed to bring her – us – good luck. Rose, oh Rose…."

Logan put his hand on Rafe's shoulder. "Now son, this is just one piece of evidence," dropping the pendant in a small paper bag. "It doesn't have to mean a bad outcome."

There was no consolation in Logan's words. Rafe realized he couldn't go any further on the search. It would be too much. The sheriff helped him back to his feet, and together they started back towards the patrol car.

Greeley and Wood were waiting for them. When they saw Logan and Rafe, they shifted back and forth uncomfortably, saddened at the sight of Rafe - awkward in the presence of a broken man.

"We found her necklace," Logan reported to the two men. "Nothing else. How about you?"

"No sir, we saw nothing that would be helpful. Most of the trails haven't been traveled recently – just not the right time of year for people to be out here, I reckon," Wood spoke up.

They heard steps on the gravel behind them. Rafe turned to see Officers Martin and Downey approaching. Martin had a grim look on his face and a frayed scrap of yellow cloth in his hand. "We found this," he said. "Could be part of a shirt or…"

"A dress." Rafe finished Officer Martin's sentence for him. "It's Rose's dress."

"How can you be sure, son?" Logan asked him.

"I know that material well. It's the dress she wore when we told our parents about the baby. It's the dress she had on the last time I ever saw her." Rafe spoke and moved robotically now. He got into the passenger side of the patrol car and sat staring straight ahead.

"Boys, I thank you for your help," Logan said, opening another bag for Officer Martin to drop the yellow material in. "It seems like we have some more searching to do around here."

"Yes," Officer Downey answered, "but I think it will have to be by boat. We found this down near the bottom of the cliffs, near to the river. If she was up here and fell or…or jumped…we won't be able to find her any other way."

"Then can I ask y'all to help get things coordinated on your end to do just that? Search by boat? I'm taking this young man home. I'll call your commanding officer when I get back to Kinston. Can you fill him in a little bit before then?" Logan said.

"Yes, sir, we surely will." The two young policemen started towards their own squad car. Martin turned back. "We sure hate to see the direction this seems to be taking, sir."

"Me, too, son. Me too." Logan got the driver's seat and put his sunglasses on. Wood and Greeley crawled in the back again, and a somber group made their way back to Kinston.

*   *   *

The rest of the week was a blur to Rafe. Rose's body was found by the Seven Springs police. They had taken a boat out on the Neuse and scoured the shorelines, finding Rose in a tangle of tree roots, river grass, and rocks. Rafe heard reports that she was bloated and bruised, that she was barely recognizable, and that Daisy had collapsed when she and Ham had to identify Rose's body. Rose had to be examined by the coroner before any funeral could take place; they had to rule out foul play so Logan could close the investigation.

No surprise to Logan, Rose's death was determined to be a suicide.

Glenn, Anne, and Rafe went to the funeral home together. The Caswells had many friends and the Whitfields hoped they might be able to slip in and out without too much fuss. Glenn and Anne thought Rafe was on the edge and couldn't deal with any commotion from Ham; confrontations now would help nothing.

They walked into the funeral home, signed the guest register, and proceeded straight to the front of the room where Rose lay. Ham was engaged in a discussion at the back of the room, and Daisy was sitting in a chair, facing the casket. She stared straight ahead, not moving a muscle. Anne went to her, but Glenn and Rafe approached Rose's casket.

Rafe looked at the girl he had loved so much. Despite the undertaker's efforts, she was barely recognizable now, and he tried to remember her great beauty, her love of life. What if they had controlled themselves? There would have been no baby, no sadness. They'd be at State now, talking about history and philosophy and complaining about professors. They'd be thinking about getting married. He wouldn't be here looking at a dead girl lying on pink tufted crepe. He felt Glenn elbow him, so he looked up. Ham Caswell was approaching, striding toward them like a man on a mission.

"I'm surprised you all would even come here," he started, but Glenn stopped him.

"Ham," Glenn said quietly, "hold your horses. No matter what, you can never take away the fact that these two kids loved each other, whether you liked it or not. We just wanted to pay our respects. We're sorry for the loss of Rose. We're leaving right now. Come on, son."

Ham headed for his friends at the back of the room again. Rafe and Glenn turned to Daisy and Anne. Anne was giving Daisy a hug when Glenn said, "We have to leave, honey, before it gets ugly."

"I want to pray for Rose. I'm not leaving till I do." She went to the coffin, kneeled, and began to pray silently. Glenn sat down to offer Daisy sympathy, and Rafe went to stand by his mom. While Anne prayed, he reached into his pocket, pulled something out, and leaned down to kiss Rose on the forehead; in this position, he placed Rose's four-leaf clover pendant under the pillow beneath her head. "For luck," he whispered, "though where you're going now, my love, you won't need it." When he stood upright, he helped his mother to her feet and noticed Hamilton Caswell glancing in their direction. He hoped Ham hadn't noticed his activity.

Rose's funeral was the next day. The Whitfield family did not attend. The house was quiet and solemn until 2 p.m. when the pealing of church bells startled them all. The funeral was over. Rose would be on her way to her final resting place beside Stuart in Westview Cemetery, where most of the Caswell clan was buried.

Rafe sat on the front porch. It was a cool late February day, and for a minute he wished he'd worn a sweatshirt. But then, in some way, the cool air felt cleansing. He said a quick prayer for Rose, then got up to go back in the house to call Jim Fussell at the Daily Free Press.

26

"Ham, if you don't stop drinking today, you're going to die. And I mean you'll die soon." Doc Benson was grim-faced. His demeanor was professional, and Ham met his eye with his own steady gaze.

"I don't rightly care. Stuart is gone. My little Rosebud is gone. Daisy is about half out of her gourd. There's really no one left who can handle the estate." Ham stated these things factually, as if he were talking about someone else altogether.

"You do have an heir out there. Don't you want to try to find her?" Doc Benson countered.

"That child is in another life. I hope it's a good one, but she's not a Caswell. No, I'm not interested in finding her." Ham had long ago written off his grandchild.

"Well, you don't have to listen to me, but if I were in your shoes, knowing I had a grandchild out there somewhere would be eating me up inside. I'd have to go down every road I could to try to find her. Are you sure this isn't part of why you're drinking so much, Ham? I've been your doctor for a long time, and I've never seen you in a state like this. For your information, your liver function tests are showing just how bad it's gotten, so you can't deny it to me."

"You're right. I don't have to listen to you. Just what in tarnation would I do with a child now, anyway? How would I go about introducing myself? 'Hi, I'm your long-lost grandfather who made your mother give you up for adoption.' What could I tell her about her mother? How would I explain that her own father never even got to see her?" Ham was resolute. "No, it has to be this way. I'm sure she's in a fine home and she doesn't need anyone coming along to upset the apple cart."

"Have you told the young man anything about the child?" Doc Benson prodded.

"No. I can't abide the sight of him," Ham said. "And why isn't he in Viet Nam, anyway?"

"Because he's 4-F, that's why. Heart murmur. Ham, don't you see that all this is chewing you up inside? I've known you a long time. I'm not just your doctor – I'm your friend, and I think this is killing you, I really do. Where is the child anyway?"

"Adopted by a family who lives in Idaho. I don't know their names or any other thing about them. I can tell you that the Weingarten home said it was a good family, well-to-do with some sort of mining business. They were a family who would be able to provide appropriately for the child." Ham had a self-satisfied look about this outcome.

"Well, you ought to at least tell the Whitfield boy that the baby is all right, shouldn't you? Hasn't he been tortured enough by now?"

Hamilton glared at the physician.

"I can see you have your mind made up. I'll say no more about it. I'll just remind you that as your physician, I have a responsibility to protect you, even if it's from yourself. You must stop drinking, Ham; that is, unless you *want* to die."

Ham closed his eyes for a second. He wasn't sure he minded the thought of dying. He had never been afraid of death…only the manner of death.

"If I die, how will it be, Doc? And how long do I have?"

"There are a couple of things that can happen, none of it pleasant. Right now, I can't predict with certainty how long you have or exactly how it will be for you, but this I can tell you…cirrhosis and hepatic failure never come to a peaceful end." Doc put his hand on Ham's shoulder. "You can't reverse course, but you can slow down the progression of this thing. That's how you can prolong your life. Stop drinking, Ham…for God's sake, stop drinking." He picked up Ham's chart and left the room.

As Ham buttoned up his shirt, he thought about what his long-time confidant had said. Stop drinking or die. If he stopped drinking, it would kill him anyhow, so what would be the point?

Ham left the office and walked out to the Cadillac. The June sun was blazing, and the humidity was stifling. New weather records would be set today. The inside of the car felt like an oven. He turned the key and cranked up the air conditioner. He sat for a minute, waiting for the car to cool down, then slowly pulled out of the parking lot, thinking about what Doc Benson had said about finding the child. He had heard that the Whitfield boy had been hunting for her…he wondered how much progress Rafe had made. He hesitated too long at a stop light. A honking horn from the car behind him interrupted his thoughts and locked in a decision. He turned and started over to the Kinston Free Press without any real sense of exactly why he was going or what he was going to do once he got there.

As he parked on the street across from the newspaper office, he had a moment of regret, a feeling he was not used to. What was he thinking? This might be one of the most ill-considered things he had ever done. He waited for a minute before exiting the car and walking across the street.

Ham opened the door to the Free Press office and a young lady glanced up from a reception desk.

"May I help you?" asked the young woman.

"I'm here to see Rafe Whitfield. Is he around?" Ham was surprised at how easily these words came from his lips.

"Why yes, he is here right now. Can I have your name, please, and I'll fetch him." She smiled sweetly at Ham. She reminded him of his little Rose, and for a moment, he almost turned and walked right back out.

"I'm Hamilton Caswell," he said quietly.

"Ok, Mr. Caswell. Just have a seat." The girl pointed to a wood, hard-back chair along the wall and disappeared down a hall. She clearly had no idea who he was.

Ham walked around in the office a little. It looked much the same as it did when it was built. He looked at framed newspapers from years gone by. On one wall, he found an article with Rafe's name in the byline. He read the first few paragraphs and found that the boy had a surprisingly good way with words.

It seemed like it was taking a long time. Maybe Rafe wouldn't even see him. He started to walk towards the door, then stopped. He had come this far. He had never run from a difficult conversation. He sat down in the wood chair.

The young lady reappeared. "Mr. Caswell, Mr. Whitfield is on the phone, but he expects to be done soon and will see you then. Can you wait for a couple of minutes?"

"Yes," Ham replied. He looked down at his watch and wondered again if this was a mistake. Before he could raise his eyes, he heard a voice he hadn't heard in a long while.

"Good afternoon, Mr. Caswell. Why don't you come on back to my office?" Rafe Whitfield was standing before him, offering his hand. Ham was surprised, but extended his own shaky hand to Rafe. He was sure Rafe could see the palsy that had set in.

He followed Rafe back to a small but comfortable office. The desk was neatly organized. There was a picture of Rafe and Rose in a small silver frame on the corner of a bookshelf. Ham picked it up and looked at it for a moment, then set it carefully back on the shelf.

"Please sit down," Rafe said. "I guess you can imagine that I'm surprised to see you."

"Probably no more surprised than I am to be here," Ham started. "I'm not sure what compelled me, but since I found myself at your doorstep, I figured I may as well come talk to you." Ham took a deep breath and thought for a minute about what he wanted to say next. Rafe kept his eyes on Ham and never looked away.

"Boy, I am going to die." He saw Rafe's shock and quickly continued. "It's not a big deal. I'm not afraid to die. At this point, I almost welcome it."

"When did you find this out?" Rafe spoke in a gentle tone. No matter what had gone before, he was kind in the face of calamity.

"My doctor just told me today. I drink too much, as you probably know, and it's killing me, slowly but surely." Ham seemed almost defiant about this.

Rafe thought for a minute about Stuart Caswell's fate. Two peas in a pod, they were. "Mr. Caswell, are they sure? And why are you telling me this?"

"I haven't quite come to a conclusion about that, boy. However, Doc Benson has come to a conclusion about my liver...it's shot. I'm done for. Maybe that's part of why I've come to see you. I wasn't intending on seeing you again and I've not come to make any amends for the past. I'm not here for confession, to apologize, or any of that. I think I've come because I heard you have been looking for the child." Ham leaned back in his chair and narrowed his eyes. "I heard you've been looking," he repeated.

"Well, yes I have, but why would you be interested in that now?" Rafe asked, now irritated at the flippant way Hamilton Caswell approached this topic. Why did he always have to be so arrogant? "You certainly didn't have any consideration for the child when you sent her mother away. You certainly didn't have any consideration for the child when Rose was forced to give her away, which I assume is what you did. And you certainly didn't have any consideration for Rose when she got home, crazy with grief." He was aware that his voice was getting louder and that his cheeks were burning with anger. It annoyed him that Ham could still chafe him so much. "I can't believe you have the audacity to come in here and ask if I've found the child I never even had a chance to see or to love when it was all your doing that I missed the privilege in the first place." Rafe stood up. "I think it's time for you to leave, Mr. Caswell."

"Hold your horses, boy. I still think it was the right thing to do at the time. I didn't know how fragile Rose's mind would be, although I should have guessed, based on her mother's mental state. Sit down and let me tell you something. I think I can help you find some peace if you'll let me." Ham put his head back and stared at the ceiling, waiting for Rafe to answer.

Rafe sat back down and rubbed his forehead with his hands. Was he really hearing this now, after so much pain? So much heartbreak? The false lead and wasted time? He looked up at his nemesis. "Well, go ahead."

Ham looked at Rafe. "Rose never was in Chicago. That's the first thing you should know."

Rafe closed his eyes, disconsolate upon hearing it straight from the horse's mouth. "I already knew that. Where was she?"

"She was in Winchester, Virginia, at the Cordelia Weingarten Home," Ham told him.

She had only been six hours away. Rafe felt sick with grief. "Do you know the actual date of the baby's birth?" Rafe asked. "That would be a good thing for me to have known while I have been on this wild goose chase." He was disgusted, but wanted to find out all he could.

"Yes. November 11, Armistice Day. She was born on Armistice Day. Well, you know - Veteran's Day." Ham replied.

Rafe thought back for a minute. That would have put the baby's conception at about the middle of February or thereabouts...that would have been right. "Then she was born full term and without any problems?" Rafe asked.

"No. Rose got along just fine, according to the home administrator, but that baby – I suppose you should know - she died right after birth. Then Rose went crazy. Between the baby and, of course, Stu, she couldn't handle any more." Ham hoped the boy wouldn't see any evidence of this lie on his face. "Rose was weak, like her mama."

Rafe ignored the insult to the girl he had loved. "Is there anything else you'd like to say? Any more salt to rub in the wound?" he managed to spit out.

"No, I reckon that's about it. Now, at least, you can stop your searching for that baby girl. She's dead and buried wherever they put those children." Hamilton stood to leave.

Rafe ran his hand through his hair. He could barely control his anger, his grief. Right at that moment, he wished he could be the one to kill Hamilton Caswell. Instead, he composed himself, looked at Ham and said, "I'm grateful for the information. At least I know what happened." He stood up, calm and quiet. "I won't say I'm sorry about your diagnosis, Mr. Caswell. It would be disingenuous. You made my life a hell on earth. You made Rose's life a hell on earth. All because of one mistake Rose and I made."

Ham stood up, too. "No need to say you're sorry - I would have known it was a lie. I'd rather have you spit in my eye and be honest about it. I'll leave you to your business, now." Ham turned and walked to the door. Placing his hand on the doorknob, he looked back. "If I were you, I'd stop looking at the past. You must come to some kind of peace in your own life. I have just attempted to make peace for myself. I believe it's the best I can do." Then he left, closing the door quietly behind him.

Rafe sat back down in the chair. He began to shiver, as if the room had gone suddenly cold. He took a sip of coffee from a cup he had sitting on the desk, but it was cold, too.

What had he just experienced? Clearly, Ham was looking for redemption, but he was so arrogant that it hardly made sense. Maybe knowing that he was going to die had stirred up some semblance of remorse in Hamilton Caswell, though based on past experience, it seemed unlikely.

Then it occurred to Rafe that Ham might be lying. Dying or not, he was a long-time cheat and a liar. It was second nature to the man. Why should Rafe trust the old buzzard now? True or not, Ham had said Rose was in Winchester...Rafe could begin his search again, only this time for his child.

He picked up the phone and called his receptionist. "Sonya, let's close up shop today. Why don't you take the rest of the day off? Let's call it a week. No, no, I'm fine. Just tired. It's been a long week. We're in good shape for the next edition. Ok. I'll see you Monday."

Rafe hung up and sat back in his chair, closed his eyes and remembered the girl he had loved more than his own life, the girl he had wanted to marry, and the baby girl – *his* baby girl – supposedly buried in some unknown pauper's cemetery; and if she *wasn't* buried, maybe there was hope, after all.

He stood up, grabbed his suit jacket, and left the office. He needed a drink, but he thought about Stuart and Hamilton Caswell and decided instead to just go straight home, have a Coke, and consider what to do next.

27

Hamilton John Caswell died on the Fourth of July, 1969, and his funeral some days later had only a few attendees. His drinking and his temper had pushed everyone in town away from him. Even those who had been his political friends and those who had worked for him were conspicuous in their absence. Only the minister, Doc Benson, Daisy, Miss Stella, Anne and Glenn were at the graveside. Rafe went, too, but at least in part because of his role in reporting significant events in the area. Whether you were friend or foe, Ham Caswell's death was news.

After the graveside prayers, Daisy approached Rafe. In a small, lace-gloved hand, she held a single rose that she had pulled off the top of the casket. "Rafe," she said, "why don't you come over this afternoon for a little while? I'd like to talk to you if I may, and this just isn't the place."

Rafe agreed to be at her home at 3 p.m. He drove home with his parents in silence until Anne finally asked, "What did Daisy want, Rafe?"

"She wants me to come over for a little while. She wants to talk. I imagine she wants to have some kind of soul-cleansing." He was cynical these days. Too much had happened.

"You don't have to go, son," said Glenn. "That family has done nothing but make your life miserable. I can't imagine what Daisy would have to say that could make it any better at this point."

Rafe thought for a minute. "Well, she really had nothing to do with sending Rose away, we know that. It was all Ham's doing. She didn't stand up for her daughter like she should have, but she's always seemed to be as much a victim as Rose was, and I'm going to go. I don't know if I can ever find any resolution, but I have to try. Maybe this is part of that process." They all fell silent and didn't speak anymore even after they had arrived at home.

Rafe ate a sandwich and went up to his old room. He laid down on the bed and looked up at the ceiling, as he had done so many times as a kid, thinking about his future. Everything he had dreamed all those years ago had gone bad.

At the appointed time, Rafe got in his car and drove out to the Caswell estate. Miss Stella opened the door for him before he had even reached the porch."

"I'm glad to see you, boy," she said.

"I'm glad to see you, too, Miss Stella," Rafe replied.

"Miz Caswell is in the sittin' room. You know where to go," the old woman said.

"Yes. Yes, I certainly do."

Rafe entered the sitting room and saw Daisy in a rocker by the window. She was watching hummingbirds at a feeder. Rafe cleared his throat to make his presence known, and she turned.

"Rafe, come over here and sit down. Look at these beautiful little creatures," Daisy said.

Rafe found another chair near the window and joined Daisy. "Aren't they amazing?" Daisy asked. "I've always loved hummingbirds...they're so tiny and fragile-looking, yet they fly all the way to Mexico every fall. Did you know that?"

"No ma'am, I didn't. I don't know much about hummingbirds," Rafe replied.

"Well, I've read about them quite a bit. Many times I've wished I could fly away with them." She paused, chewing her bottom lip for a minute. "Rafe, what Ham didn't know about his family was that he could not instill in them the strength he had. Stu was not strong. Rose was not strong. But Ham underestimated me. Mind you, he never loved me. For years he abused me, both mentally and physically, thinking he could break me. I've never had anywhere to turn but here." She looked back out at the hummingbirds. "I've known what Ham could never figure out...that you only have to be strong enough to keep your wings moving."

And Daisy was just strong enough, Rafe thought to himself, watching her rock.

They sat in silence for a few minutes, watching the tiny birds, hovering and drinking, zipping away, then returning for more nectar.

Daisy turned to him. "I'm sorry for all you've been through, I truly am. I was powerless to do anything but hold on – keep my wings moving. And now here I am; I made it, but I'm all alone and I surely never anticipated that. I do hope your mother and daddy will stop out and visit sometimes."

"I'm sure they will. You have a lot of friends at church and in the community, too," Rafe answered.

She laughed bitterly. "I have a lot of acquaintances but few friends."

"Then maybe you can start all over," Rafe said, standing up to leave.

"And perhaps that's what you should do, too...start over," Daisy replied. A stifling, heavy silence came over them for a minute, then Daisy added, "Thank you for coming. I wasn't sure you really would, and I appreciate it. You would have been a good husband for Rose, wouldn't you?"

Rafe sighed. "I like to think so. Good-bye, Mrs. Caswell." Then he turned and walked out into the foyer. Miss Stella was nowhere to be seen. He would have liked to thank her for her years of kindness. He knew he would never be back.

He walked out the front door. The sky was overcast with dark gray clouds. It was an unusually cool day for this time of year, but he suddenly felt hot; he was perspiring as if it was a hundred degrees. He sat down on the steps of the house.

Miss Stella opened the door behind him and came out. She walked down the steps and sat down by Rafe, pulling a sweater close around her.

"Are you all right, Mr. Rafe? You need a glass of water?" Miss Stella asked.

"No, Miss Stella, but thank you for checking on me. I just felt like I had to sit here a minute," he replied, placing his hands on his thighs and sitting up straight, trying to shake off the dizziness that had momentarily overcome him.

Miss Stella sat quietly by him, and they both looked down the long lane that lead out to the main road. After a minute, she turned to him, put one of her knobby-fingered hands over his and said, "You've walked a ragged road, son - a mighty ragged road. Your heart has been broke in too many pieces, hain't it?"

Rafe choked up at her compassion. "Yes. And sometimes I don't know if it'll ever come back together."

"You got to *make* it come back together. You got to git on 'bout your life. Don't let this shadow hang over you; turn your face up to the sun, boy." She paused, pulled her hand away and said, "Go on, now. There ain't nothin' roun' here but sorrow." She stood up, and he stood up with her. She walked up the steps, turning just as she reached the door.

"Good-bye, boy."

Rafe got into his car and drove down that long driveway one last time. He went to the newspaper office and sat down in the chair behind his desk. For all that had happened, he still had to get the Free Press out to the subscribers.

He looked at the picture on his bookshelf of him and Rose, and it felt like a lifetime had passed. His heartbreak was no longer like a knife, but a deep sadness, persistently pulling at his insides. He thought about what Melissa had once said to him. The next generation of young women and men were doomed to repeat his grief. But what should be done? He felt inadequate to the task.

There was a lot of work on his desk, but he couldn't focus on it right at that moment. Instead, he took a clean piece of paper, placed it into his typewriter and began tapping the keys. Once he started the motion of typing, the words began to flow, his pain spilling out onto the paper in black ink, and it was oddly satisfying...

Old timers believe the Neuse River has heard the secrets, cries, and laughter of young and old, swallowing confidences into the muddy bottom. Joys and heartaches of generations have washed into the water to be swept away or crashed on the rocks. The river leaves nothing behind....

ABOUT THE AUTHOR

Theresa Konwinski is a wife, mom, and retired registered nurse. She enjoys a variety of activities, only one of which is writing. Her first novel, *An Extraordinary Year,* was published in 2016.

www.ingramcontent.com/pod-product-compliance
Lightning Source LLC
Chambersburg PA
CBHW051832090426
42736CB00011B/1770